The Blind Men and the Elephant

and other essays in biographical criticism

Bernth Lindfors

Africa World Press, Inc.

P.O. Box 1892
Trenton, NJ 08607

P.O. Box 48
Asmara, ERITREA

Africa World Press, Inc.

First Printing 1999

Cover design: Jonathan Gullery

Library of Congress Cataloging-in-Publication Data

Lindfors, Bernth.
The blind men and the elephant and other essays in biographical criticism / Bernth Lindors.
p. cm.
Includes bibliographical references and index.
ISBN 0-86543-728-9 (hb). -- ISBN 0-86543-729-7 (pb)
1. African literature (English)--History and criticism.
2. Authors, African--20th century--Biography. 3. Africa--Intellectual life--20th century. I. Title.
PR9340.5.L56 1999
820.9'896--dc21
[B] 98-55999
CIP

Table of Contents

Preface to the Second Edition

The first edition of this book, published in Adelaide by the Centre for Research in the New Literatures in English at the Flinders University of South Australia, did not circulate widely in Africa or the West. The purpose of this new edition is to make these essays more readily available to the audiences for which they were intended. One new essay, on reactions in Nigeria to Amos Tutuola's death, has been added. All the rest are reprinted here with only minor editorial emendations.

I wish to thank Stacey Peebles for careful computer scanning, proofreading, and indexing, and Cinde Hastings for preparing the final camera-ready copy of this book with characteristic professional efficiency.

Introduction

In an intellectual climate dominated by formalistic theoretical concerns, biographical criticism may seem an unfashionable mode of academic discourse. The New Critics, the Structuralists and now the Deconstructionists, by focusing intently on the internal dynamics of a text, have depersonalized modern literary studies by ignoring the author behind the text, claiming that he or she is irrelevant to their analytical pursuits. What matters to such expert explicators is the logistics underlying an arrangement of words on a page, not the life and times of the individual who happened to set those words down. Indeed, it is often asserted that a work of literature has an existence of its own, quite independent of that of its creator. The writer is merely a proficient midwife, a distraction, and a bore. Why should anyone today take an interest in examining something as old-fashioned as the relationship between a human being and a literary text?

The best answer may have been given more than two hundred and fifty years ago by Alexander Pope: The proper study of mankind is man. Literature, one of man's most interesting creations, certainly is worthy of rigorous scrutiny, but even the most exacting literary scholarship will be of little value if it does not ultimately lead us to a better understanding of ourselves and others. Although verbal constructs may be fascinating to contemplate solely for their own sake, they remain human products, and as such, cannot be comprehended fully until they have been traced back to a specific human source in a particular human environment. The text, in other words, is so completely conditioned by its shaping context that it cannot be adequately grasped and appreciated without some knowledge of its creator and the circumstances that prompted its creation. Biographical criticism, by studying the human face behind the text, may assist us in the larger task of reading our fellow man.

This kind of criticism is sorely needed when writers and readers hail from different cultures. Western readers of nonwestern literatures sometimes need supplementary cultural information in order to come to terms with unfamiliar social issues embedded in a novel, play or poem. They may also require a good glossary of local terms. But the problem isn't simply a matter of translation. People literally poles apart who happen to speak the same language may not share the same semantics or the same world view, so one may believe he understands the other when he does not. The significance of certain actions or statements in a foreign literary work may escape him totally, leading him to misinterpret the drama being enacted before him. Biographical criticism may help such a reader enter the world of the author more completely and make better sense of what he finds there.

The essays in this book approach African literary subjects from a variety of biographical perspectives. The first two deal with biographical criticism itself, offering examples of how it can be abused as a method of literary evaluation. The next three are concerned with demonstrating why the themes and techniques employed by Dennis Brutus, Wole Soyinka and Ngugi wa Thiong'o have changed significantly over time. The remaining essays are primarily biographical, setting down a reliable factual record of important moments in the careers of two African writers, a German scholar and a South African performer. Each essay has its own strategy, but they all work toward a common goal: illumination of a reciprocity between literature and life.

All of these essays have been published previously, and I would like to thank the editors of *Africa* (Rome), *African Literature*

Association Bulletin, African Literature Today, West Africa, West African Journal of Modern Languages, Yale French Studies, World Literature Written in English, Peuples Noirs/Peuples Africains, Journal of Commonwealth Literature, Neo-African Literature and Culture and *The Commonwealth Writer Overseas* for allowing me to reprint them here. I also wish to thank the Graduate School and the University Research Institute of The University of Texas at Austin for providing a generous publication subsidy. And of course I am extremely grateful to Syd Harrex and CRNLE's publications committee for the kindness they have shown to this blind man and his elephant.

The Blind Men and the Elephant

There is a famous story about six blind men encountering an elephant for the first time. Each man, seizing on the single feature of the animal which he happened to have touched first, and being incapable of seeing it whole, loudly maintained his limited opinion on the nature of the beast. The elephant was variously like a wall, a spear, a snake, a tree, a fan or a rope, depending on whether the blind men had first grasped the creature's side, tusk, trunk, knee, ear, or tail.[1]

I have referred to this fable because I believe it epitomizes the problem of every critic who is confronted with a new work of art, especially one that comes out of a culture different from his own. It is impossible for him to see the thing whole. He may inspect it with the greatest curiosity and scholarly care, counting its parts, studying its structure, analyzing its texture, probing its private recesses, measuring its real and symbolic dimensions, and trying to weigh its ultimate significance, but he will never master all its complexity, never understand everything that makes it live and move as an independent artistic creation. He simply cannot help but perceive it from his own limited point of view which has been conditioned by his previous cultural experiences. In a desperate effort to make some sense of unfamiliar lines and contours he may resort to comparisons with other forms he knows quite well, drawing parallels where oblique coincidences happen to intersect. The elephant thus becomes a wall, a spear, a snake, a tree, a fan, a rope. And the blind men bicker about the accuracy of their perceptions while truth stands huge and unrecognized in their midst.

The native critic, it has been argued, is better equipped than anyone else to appreciate the creative genius of his own culture. He is the only one who can grab the elephant by the tail and still look him straight in the eye. He is able to achieve this partly because he was born and bred closest to the beastly truth and partly because his upbringing has endowed him with superior insight into the workings of his society, the ground upon which this truth stands. Yet it would seem obvious that anyone so close to what he is viewing would have trouble viewing it in a larger context and assessing it with the kind of dispassionate objectivity that rational aesthetic evaluation requires. Indeed, if all interpretation were left to native critics, truth might be sought principally on a local level, its universal dimensions all but forgotten. Common sense just does not allow a single tribe of critics to claim a monopoly on clear vision. Every individual will have his blind spots, and some critics—native as well as foreign—will be much blinder than others.

This is why any literature needs all the criticism it can get. Only by glimpsing truth from a variety of perspectives are we able to comprehend its complexities and ambiguities. Only by comparing different views of the same subject can we arrive at a valid conception of what it really looks like. If we choose to stand still and see everything through rose-colored spectacles, we will have a narrow, tainted vision of reality. Our image of the elephant will be incomplete and distorted by our bias.

If we could learn to accept the fact that no individual—not even the author himself—is capable of telling the whole truth and nothing but the truth about a literary work, we would then be in a better position to evaluate the contribution a critic makes to our understanding of that work. We would not expect perfection, for we would realize that literary criticism is a fickle and uncertain art in which no-one has the final word. There are never any right or wrong answers as in elementary mathematics or physics; there are only good and bad arguments based on different interpretations of the same data.

The critic who ventures to criticize other critics must therefore not only be aware of his own perceptual limitations and guard against acute astigmatism and myopia, but he must also take pains to build a sound case for his particular point of view. It is not enough for him to swagger and shout insults at everyone who sees things differently. He must be sure of his footing before he casts his spear, and he must aim carefully if he wants to hit his target squarely. Above all, he must refrain from launching irrelevant personal attacks for his quarrel is not with men but with their ideas. One cannot restore a blind man's vision by flogging him.

To illustrate polar extremes of good and bad metacriticism (defined here as criticism of literary criticism) one need look no farther than *African Literature Today*, No. 5 (1971). 1 will select two articles, both of which happen to challenge views I expressed in earlier issues of the same journal. Ernest Emenyonu, in a provocative essay entitled "African Literature: What does it take to be its critic?" (1-11) takes me to task for having a low opinion of Cyprian Ekwensi's art[2] and Gareth Griffiths, in "Language and Action in the Novels of Chinua Achebe" (88-105), questions my assertions about Achebe's use of proverbs.[3] Let us look at Emenyonu's complaints first.

Emenyonu obviously admires Ekwensi both as a literary artist and as a man. He knows him personally, has interviewed him extensively about his life and writings, and is convinced that "both the characters and settings of his novels are truly African" (7). He also seems persuaded that if I and other "Western critics" only knew Ekwensi personally, would take the trouble to interview him extensively about his life and writings, and would try to become acquainted with the diverse African peoples and places upon which he bases his novels, then we too would be genuinely impressed with his literary genius. Indeed, until we are willing to make this investment in intimacy, we are incapable of judging him fairly, for "even well-intentioned minds" will be misled by "inadequate information" (4). Any of Ekwensi's close friends and associates would presumably be a better critic of his works than a total stranger who has never met him socially. To bolster his argument, Emenyonu offers bits and pieces of biographical data which are intended to help us understand and appreciate Ekwensi's craftsmanship. Some of this information can be found on dust jackets of Ekwensi's novels and would be very difficult for anyone remotely interested in his work to overlook. The fact that Ekwensi has had a varied career as a "teacher, a journalist, a forestry officer, a pharmacist, a broadcaster, a features producer, a film writer, a dramatist, a national director of Information Services, head of a national broadcasting corporation, and a diplomat" is too well known to bear repeating, but the sequence in which he held these jobs while developing as a writer is, as Emenyonu rightly maintains, of vital importance to any investigation of his literary evolution. It therefore seems odd that Emenyonu should reject my attempts "to prove something about the gap between Ekwensi's publication dates and the actual dates when the author wrote the works" (6). I was not, as he states later, "trying to assess Ekwensi's artistic growth from the chronological order of the publication of his works" (7) but rather from the chronological order in which the works were *written*. In other words, I was attempting to do precisely what Emenyonu himself insists the responsible critic must do: establish a factual basis for generalizations about an author's development. It is true I had no way of knowing that "the raw materials for *People of the City* had been collected as far back as 1947" (7),[4] but I knew from delving into Ekwensi's background that the book had been written on a brief boat trip to England. However, according to three printed sources based on early interviews with the author,[5] this trip took place in 1951, not 1953 as Emenyonu claims! If Emenyonu is so intent on setting the biographical record straight, one wishes he would make an effort to verify the "facts" he collected from Mr. Ekwensi.

Another surprising inconsistency in Emenyonu's argument is his unwillingness to accept certain kinds of biographical evidence. That Ekwensi has been influenced by many types of

Western literature is a fact that even Ekwensi himself would not dispute. Indeed, in 1964 he published an autobiographical essay entitled "Literary Influences on a Young Nigerian" (*Times Literary Supplement*, 4 June 1964, pp. 475-476) in which he cited no fewer than twenty Western writers who had made some impact on him. In interviews he has mentioned still others as being "always present in my imagination when I write."[6] It therefore seems very peculiar that my efforts to document the extent of Ekwensi's debt to certain of these sources should be treated by Emenyonu with scornful sarcasm. Why are some well-established biographical facts admissible and others not? Emenyonu would have us believe that

> *the only thing that should be known* about Ekwensi in this regard is that he had an early overpowering and almost compulsive interest in reading, especially fiction. So possessed was Ekwensi by this trait that even while his teachers were solving mathematical equations on the blackboard, Ekwensi was preoccupied with novels hidden between his legs beneath his desk. (6. Italics mine)

If this interesting bit of gossip is truly the "only thing that should be known" about Ekwensi's reading habits, why should anyone do any further research on the subject? Emenyonu seems to want to set rigid limits on certain kinds of biographical inquiry even while demanding that critics do their utmost to learn everything there is to know about the life and times of the author.

Curiously enough, some of the statements Emenyonu makes do more to support my contentions about Ekwensi than they do to refute them. For instance, his remark that "any other West African who went through the unfortunately British dominated educational system read virtually the same titles as Ekwensi" (6), reveals that Ekwensi was more profoundly influenced by certain books than were his contemporaries who had equal access to them. Otherwise, why would not more authors in British West Africa have written like Rider Haggard, Robert Louis Stevenson and Edgar Wallace? Why was Ekwensi the only one who produced juvenile adventure fiction of this indelible stamp? The answer seems to be that the others outgrew their interest in popular schoolboy classics while Ekwensi was still strongly under their spell, at least in the earliest phase of his career. There may be better explanations, but however one chooses to interpret the evidence, the fact remains that Ekwensi copied familiar foreign models which other African writers consciously or unconsciously eschewed. As an imitator of Western adolescent adventure fiction, he was unique.

What is more bizarre about Emenyonu's argument is his assumption that there is some kind of conspiracy among Western critics to denigrate the works of African authors who opt to write about "the Africa of today, under the influence of today's economic pressures, politics, and conflict of values" (6). He asserts that most Western critics prefer novels and plays set deep in the bush because these works reflect "African primitive ways" and therefore yield the type of ethnographic and sociological data that people ignorant of contemporary African realities are invariably looking for (2). If an African author defies the expectations of these prejudiced critics by writing about modern times, he is branded un-African, and if he happens to write well, he is immediately suspected of having some Western literary blood in his veins and the critics begin a frantic search for his European or American ancestors (2-3). One wonders if Emenyonu really believes in the malevolent bogeymen he has termed "Western critics" in this imaginative scenario, or if he is merely trying to erect a racial barrier behind which he can hide suspect defensive criticism. For the strategy is quite clever. If we accept Emenyonu's premises and endorse his demonology, we are then forced to conclude (1) that any non-African who finds fault with an African literary work set in "the Africa of today" is a narrow-minded primitivist with his heart in the jungle, and (2) any non-African who seeks to identify traces of Western influence in an African novel, play, or poem is a hardened racist incapable of explaining African literary creativity in any other way. The *deus ex machina* in this black and white morality play is of course the African critic whom Emenyonu heralds as "more disposed to offer [his] views on an African work solely to help the reader towards gaining a *proper perspective* of the author and the realities of his work" (10. Italics mine). Only a blind man of a special hue can see the elephant properly and tell the world what it really looks like!

More disturbing than the latent xenophobia underlying Emenyonu's argument is his tendency to tar many Western critics with the same brush. I cannot pretend to know as much about the motives and morals of Anne Tibble, A.G. Stock, and Austin Shelton as Emenyonu claims to know, but I can at least answer some of the charges he levels at me. First, I want to assure him that I am not hopelessly infatuated with village novels depicting "African primitive ways." I happen to think that the urban novels of Soyinka, Armah, and Awoonor are among the best to have come out of Africa; I prize them not because they are "modern" in setting, theme, and technique, but because they are extraordinarily perceptive and beautifully written. I admire Achebe's rural novels for the same reason: they are elegant works of art. Secondly, my interest in African literature is more literary than anthropological, sociological, or racialistic. I do not particularly care what Africans choose to write about so long as they write well. Thirdly, I do not believe that "a Peace Corps sojourn, a spell of field work in Africa, a conference in African literature, a graduate studentship in African literature in a Western university, any of these is enough to qualify one as an authority on African literature" (10). Nor do I believe that "African literature in all its ramifications represents a mere appendage to British or French literature since most of the African writers write chiefly in English or French" (1). I am sure these notions are as repugnant to me as they are to Emenyonu. Finally, my effort to detect foreign (and native!) influences on Ekwensi's writing was not a back-handed maneuver to explain away his successes but a straightforward attempt to account for his failures. I sincerely doubt that I will think more highly of Ekwensi as a literary artist "as soon as [he] writes a novel about black magic, ritual, medicine men, mud and thatched huts, banana leaves, palm trees and rolling rivers" (6-7). After all, Ekwensi tried this years ago in at least two of his school readers—*Juju Rock* and *The Leopard's Claw*—and in sections of *Jagua Nana*.

All these points would have been clear to Emenyonu if he had been able to suppress his fears about Western critics plotting the overthrow of modern African literature or if he had simply known me and my critical writings better. Why should the courtesy of elementary biographical research be extended only to creative writers and not to critics?

One legitimate answer to this question is that biographical research really doesn't matter at all because it is totally irrelevant to literary evaluation. A writer must be judged by what he writes, not by how he lives. Interviews and other forms of biographical inquiry may be interesting ways to collect personal information about an author but they are not substitutes for intelligent appraisal of his works. This applies to novelists as well as critics. The fact that Ekwensi was a poor student of mathematics does not make him a great writer. The fact that he has had a diversified career does not guarantee that his novels will be successful. Although we cannot prevent fascinating personal revelations from conditioning our attitude towards an artist, we should never allow them to determine our response to his art. Literary biography must not usurp the function of literary criticism.

Following this train of thought, one is tempted to go a step further and postulate that the least reliable critics are likely to be those who know an author personally, for their feelings towards him as a man will subvert their critical objectivity. It would be very difficult for any close friend or lifelong enemy of an artist to view his art with scholarly detachment. Even those who know him only slightly are apt to hold firm opinions about him which will color their reactions to what he creates. This is one of the great dangers of conducting biographical research with a tape recorder. The interviewer who interrogates the author face to face is bound to come away with a vivid impression of his character and personality, and this impression will linger and influence him when he sits down to evaluate the writer's work. If we accept Emenyonu's dictum that African literature "should be looked at objectively or not at all" (10), logic dictates that we must reject all criticism by friends, acquaintances, and interviewers of African authors. *Ergo,* we must reject Emenyonu's assessment of Ekwensi.

I admit this is an extreme position and not one which I would choose to defend with my last drop of ink. I happen to believe that biographical research is a valid and useful mode of literary investigation and that interviews are essential for eliciting an author's conception of his own work. But I do not believe that biographical criticism provides all the answers to problems of literary interpretation nor that it even necessarily raises the most meaningful questions about an author and his books. For the biographical critic is as limited in vision as anyone else and as prone to see the universe from a single point of view. If he is not aware that the author he is studying is equally crippled in insight and perception, then he is likely to be rather arrogant in his assertions, insisting that there is only one *proper perspective* on the truth. He will not realize that he and the author are only two blind men among many who seek to explain the mystery of the elephant by viewing it from a certain angle.

Before leaving this subject, let me say that I agree with Emenyonu that too little biographical research has been done on African authors, but I am not inclined to blame this deficiency primarily on Western critics. It seems to me that African scholars are in the best position to do this type of research, especially if they share a common cultural heritage with a prominent author.

As far as metacriticism is concerned, I hope it is clear that I am not arguing that critics should avoid challenging opinions with which they disagree. Critical debates are necessary not only to correct misinformation but also, more vitally, to clarify points of view which are in conflict. Metacriticism justifies itself only by contributing something new and original to literary interpretation.

An example of good metacriticism is Gareth Griffiths's "Language and Action in the Novels of Chinua Achebe," which argues that Achebe's verbal artistry is far more subtle and complex than is generally recognized, even by critics who admire his excellence as a stylist. Griffiths points out that because Achebe is a master of irony and ambiguity, one cannot accept every statement in his fiction at its face value. There are likely to be extra nuances of meaning embedded in a word, phrase, or sentence, depending on where, when, how, why, and by whom it is uttered. This is especially true of proverbs, which must be studied in context before their full significance can be understood and appreciated.

Griffiths therefore takes issue with my contention that Achebe's proverbs, examined in isolation, provide a "grammar of values" by which the deeds of characters can be measured and evaluated. Griffiths insists we must watch how these proverbs operate within the larger lexicon of rhetoric built into the novels before we can attach moral meaning to them. The proverbs cannot be trusted to deliver only one message; their environment and semantic elasticity may give them strange new shapes, abnormal connotations. Moreover, Achebe himself is at pains to prove that the old "proverbial culture itself...no longer provides a valid morality [because] the proverbial universe is no longer intact (93)...the moral universe of the proverbs with its sequence of appropriate actions and responses has disintegrated along with the society which produced it" (97). By employing proverbs ironically, Achebe thus reinforces a major historical point central to all his novels.

This is a persuasive argument, and I am willing to accept most of it without question. Griffiths has exposed serious limitations in my approach to Achebe's proverbs and has offered an attractive alternative mode of analysis which he demonstrates can yield significant insights into the nature of Achebe's genius as a writer. His penetrating observations on "proverbial patterning" and aesthetic distance help to advance our understanding of the extraordinarily complex web of social and linguistic relationships that Achebe creates in his fiction. Yet I am not entirely convinced that Griffiths's analytical procedures are basically different from my own or that they always lead him in the best direction. Proverbs are perhaps too slippery to be grasped by one hand, no matter how deft and dexterous that hand might be.

In examining Achebe's proverbs out of context, I was attempting to study them as independent resonators of moral ideas which gained amplification through frequency of sounding. The more often a particular note was heard, the more important it became in the total concert of meaning Achebe was orchestrating. The context didn't matter so much as the repeated occurrence of the same sound throughout the artistic performance, because it was through constant bombardment that the composer communicated major moral ideas to his audience.

My method of analysis could hardly be called original. Anyone who has spent time tracking down "image clusters" in a Shakespearean play, dominant symbols in a poem, or recurring motifs in a novel has done essentially the same kind of work. It involves extracting the data from the text, organizing it into logical categories, and then commenting on the significance of its patterns. It is basically an inductive technique requiring that the investigator examine a large quantity of evidence before venturing to draw conclusions.

Griffiths rejects context-free proverb analysis as inadequate because it fails to consider the "total linguistic structure" in which the proverbs are set (96). He prefers a method which will take into account unstated as well as stated truths, submerged as well as surface meanings. So he chooses to scrutinize the artist's words in context to see how their significations are changed by their surroundings. He is still looking for Achebe's moral message. He is still using an inductive method. The major difference between his approach and mine is that he is trying to read Achebe's meaning from a larger "grammar of values" imbedded in the novels.

To do this, he must examine the same proverbs that I examined and decide when Achebe is speaking straight and when he is talking through his *alter ego*, his ironic mask, or his hat. This is not an easy job, and the great virtue of Griffiths's essay is that he usually argues well and convincingly. But there are times when what he says neither invalidates nor differs much from what I said, even though he apparently thinks our statements are at odds. For instance, he objects to my classification of the proverb "Shall we kill a snake and carry it in our hand when we have a bag for putting long things in?" as a comment or warning "against foolish and unworthy actions." Clearly, in the context, the proverb does not warn against foolish or unworthy actions; in fact it is used by the old man at the Umuofia Progressive Union meeting to justify an unworthy action, or rather to justify an action which in terms of the tribal code is acceptable but in terms of the public morality to which Obi's position exposes him is a crime (97-98).

I would argue, also from the context, that the old man cites this proverb to condemn the foolishness of not approaching a fellow Umuofian for a special favor, particularly when he is in a good position to grant it. The old man wants Obi to use his influence to help find suitable employment for a "countryman" who has just lost his job at the Post Office. It would be foolish, indeed unworthy, of the Umuofia Progressive Union *not* to appeal to Obi, their brother in the senior service, to take the small steps necessary to remedy their compatriot's misfortune. As the old man puts it in another proverb, "that is why we say that he who has people is richer than he who has money."[7]

Griffiths is correct to note the irony of the situation—a proverbial plea for sane, responsible action is being perverted to justify an unworthy action—but this irony is visible only to the reader, not to the loyal members of the Umuofia Progressive Union. As Griffiths himself states, the proverb recommends "an action which in terms of the tribal code is acceptable." We see it differently because we stand with Achebe outside the moral universe of the average urban Umuofian, savoring its paradoxical immorality. The fact that we are in a position to appreciate a new cutting edge to an old saw does not in any way hinder the saw from continuing to operate on its original plane of significance. Indeed, the kernel notion of a "foolish and unworthy action" is amplified as much by ironic negation as by constant affirmation. The proverb still reverberates with all the appropriate thematic and moral overtones. The din is merely augmented by the mocking echo we now hear behind each articulation of the key idea. So while Griffiths is justified in calling our attention to contextual ironies which give a proverb new dimensions of meaning, he has no right to insist that we forget all the older truths it continues to convey. For these truths may endure and even prevail in the end. If *No Longer at Ease* is not a novel about foolish, unworthy actions *and their ironic consequences*, then what is it about?

Throughout his essay Griffiths pleads for recognition of the "relativity" of proverbial wisdom, pointing out that many proverbs are capable of yielding different meanings in different situations and that some become quite ambiguous if not absurd when undercut by deliberate irony. This is a good point, and one wishes Griffiths were willing to recognize a similar "relativity" in literary criticism, for sometimes he begs the question of interpretation by assuming that his opinion on a controversial text is right and others are wrong. For instance, his discussion of *A Man of the People* is based on Arthur Ravenscroft's premise that Odili is an "unreliable" hero who, in Griffiths's words,

> struggles, as far as he is able, to act up to the ideals he proposes, but despite his intentions he is betrayed time and time again into self-deception and hypocrisy. He tells his story defensively, as if half-aware of his plight, and organises his material and his comment to justify his action and its outcome. But his efforts only serve to emphasise the gap between intention and achievement. We are simultaneously made aware of the double-standards he operates when judging his own actions and those of others, and of the tragic

> innocence necessary to continue such self-deceptions successfully. (99-100)

Griffiths goes on to say that Achebe succeeds in creating an "ironic novel of high distinction" by deliberately withdrawing Odili's "capacity for honest self-appraisal" (100).

This interpretation of Odili, a further elaboration of what I would term the "Ravenscroft heresy"[8] in Achebe studies, is almost the reverse of what the author actually intended in creating his hero. If I may lapse into the somewhat uncomfortable role of biographical critic for a moment and quote what Achebe said when answering students' questions after a lecture at the University of Texas at Austin, I think the crux of the problem will be clear. Asked what his "outlook on Odili was" and whether he intended him "as an object of satire, even burlesque," Achebe answered

> Well, I like that young man. He was idealistic, he was naive, he was this and he was that, but I think he was also basically honest, which makes a difference. He was very honest. He knew his own shortcomings; he even knew when his motives were not very pure. This puts him in a class worthy of attention, as far as I'm concerned.[9]

Now if an artist views his hero as a very honest man who knows his own shortcomings, and critics tend to see the same character as a self-deceiving anti-hero incapable of honest self-appraisal, then something must be wrong either with the artist's art or with the critics' response to it. How else can the discrepancy be explained? One could perhaps try to prove that the artist was not fully aware of what he was doing, that his conception of his hero was largely an unconscious or intuitive one, and that he actually managed to create a character more complicated and therefore far more interesting than he had intended. Or one could perhaps take the opposite tack and criticize the critics for over-reacting to particular traits or deeds of the hero and consequently misinterpreting his role in the novel. Either way the discrepancy would be accounted for as a failure of perception on someone's part. One would simply have to decide whether it was the artist or the critic who was a bit obtuse.

A reasonable alternative to this sort of exegetical witchhunt would be an approach which recognized the validity of various interpretations of the same work of art, a relative approach in matters of aesthetic discrimination. Such an alternative would acknowledge that blind men are blind in different ways and none can be expected to see much beyond what is nearest to him. The literary artist is just another interpreter of the elephant who happens to be in a position to view things from the inside. This makes his perceptions no more valid or legitimate than those of any other critic. What really count are not the reactions of a single man but the accumulated impressions of generations of visually handicapped spectators. Only then will we be able to see the truth in the largest possible perspective.

If we adopt this relative approach to literary criticism, we come to realize that the stated opinions of Achebe, Griffiths, Emenyonu, and Lindfors on a given book are of no consequence in and of themselves but that they begin to assume importance when they are in substantial agreement or disagreement with what others think and say about the same book. The crucial points at issue become clear only through rational debate which focuses on the ideas rather than the personalities of the debaters. This is where Griffiths proves himself a better metacritic than Emenyonu. Instead of arguing *ad hominem*, Griffiths quarrels with the basic critical assumptions upon which my case rests and then offers another way of looking at the same data which is so perceptive and revealing that I am forced to admit the cogency of his point of view. Unlike other metacritics who would have us close our eyes so they can guide us, Griffiths tries to teach us a new way of seeing. He appears to realize that metacriticism, though a blind man's art, should be concerned with providing the clearest possible vision of literary realities.

The moral of this essay is that good metacriticism emanates from the intellect, not from the spleen, and always has as its ultimate aim a true illumination of a work of art.

NOTES

1. John Godfrey Saxe, "The Blind Men and the Elephant." *New Nation English: Book Five (B)*, ed. Etim Akaduh, et al. (London: Nelson 1968), pp. 94-96.

2. For my views on Ekwensi, see "Cyprian Ekwensi: An African Popular Novelist," *African Literature Today*, 3 (1969), 2-14.

3. For my views on Achebe's use of proverbs, see "The Palm-Oil with which Achebe's Words are Eaten," *African Literature Today*, 1 (1968), 3-18.

4. In an interview recorded in 1962 Ekwensi speaks of *People of the City* as "a little thing I turned out based on a number of short stories I wrote for Radio Nigeria." The "raw materials" had thus apparently been processed at least once before Ekwensi transmuted them into a novel. See "Cyprian Ekwensi," *African Writers Talking: A Collection of Radio Interviews*, ed. Cosmo Pieterse and Dennis Duerden (London: Heinemann; New York: Africana, 1972), p. 78.

5. *West Africa*, 21 October 1961, p. 1,157; *West African Review*, June 1956, pp. 553, 555; *Drum*, June 1952, p. 14.

6. "Entretien avec l'écrivain nigerien Cyprian Ekwensi," *Afrique*, 24 (1963), 51.

7. Chinua Achebe, *No Longer at Ease* (London: Heinemann, 1960), p. 79.

8. See Arthur Ravenscroft, "African Literature V: Novels of Disillusion," *Journal of Commonwealth Literature*, 6 (1969), 120-123.

9. "Interview with Chinua Achebe," *Palaver: Interviews with Five African Writers in Texas*, ed. Bernth Lindfors, et al. (Austin, Texas: African and Afro-American Research Institute, 1972), p. 9.

Dennis Brutus and His Critics

The poetry of Dennis Brutus has probably received less critical attention than it deserves. Considering that *Sirens Knuckles Boots* was among the first booklets of verse to be issued under the Mbari imprint in the early 1960s,[1] considering that Brutus has published ten more collections of poems since then,[2] considering that his poetic style has changed in a number of interesting ways in the forty years or so he has been actively writing, it is surprising that his work has excited so little public discussion. Other African poets who began writing at approximately the same time or later—e.g., Christopher Okigbo, Wole Soyinka, J.P. Clark, Okot p'Bitek—have already attracted a respectable body of serious commentary in books, doctoral dissertations, M.A. theses and numerous quarrelsome critical articles. But Brutus, though certainly as famous as any of his contemporaries, seems to have all but escaped such sustained scrutiny.

What accounts for this neglect? Why has Brutus been ignored by the critics? Is it because much of his poetry is so simple, so plain, so transparently lucid that it needs no laborious explication? Is it because he deals with subjects that critics are not comfortable talking about? Is it because until 1973, when *A Simple Lust* appeared, most of his work was not readily available to the reading public? Or is it because his poetry is regarded by most academic literary analysts as unworthy of close attention? Since we cannot answer such questions objectively without taking a poll of all practicing critics, perhaps we should approach the problem from a different direction by examining the remarks that have been made on his poetry in order to see where the difficulties of interpretation lie. By changing our emphasis and asking "What is the matter with Brutus's critics?" instead of "What is the matter with Brutus's poetry?" we may ultimately be able to arrive at answers to both questions.

The first critic to comment on Brutus's verse was also his first publisher Ulli Beier, the founding father of the Mbari Writers' and Artists' Club, who in an essay on "Contemporary African Poetry in English"[3] prepared for the Conference of African Writers of English Expression held at Makerere University College in Kampala in June 1962, offered a brief introduction to this new South African poet whose first collection of poems, *Sirens Knuckles Boots*, was then in the process of being assembled for publication by Mbari the following year. Though an illness prevented Beier from going to Kampala to read his paper at the conference, his remarks on Brutus were later published in both the conference proceedings and the review section of the twelfth issue of *Black Orpheus*, a high-quality literary magazine Beier edited in Nigeria. Before examining a few representative poems, Beier mentioned that Brutus, a colored student at the University of the Witwatersrand, was keenly interested in sport and had been banned by the Minister of Justice for the part he had taken in organizing a strike in 1961. Beier then went on to say:

> There is a general feeling among West African writers that South Africans indulge in continuous protest writing. They have often and severely criticised this. It has been said that they are full of self-pity and that their continuous, spineless protesting is becoming a bore and fails to arouse sympathy. The reproach is a little cheap, coming from people who have grown up without knowing any real oppression, and any real frustration. It is difficult to see how the South African writer can escape the recurring themes of race prejudice, apartheid and suppression. Some writers may have been moved to self-pity by this situation but others have certainly not.

Brutus, Beier maintained, fell into the latter category:

> Dennis Brutus often deals with political situations in his poetry, but I don't think anybody could accuse him of being self-pitying or even self-centered. On the contrary, his verse is extremely restrained and disciplined, and he speaks in a quiet, muted voice which is only possible for a person who manages to stand partly outside the events that effect [sic] him.
>
> In Dennis Brutus' verse there is none of the outcry, the scream, the anger of protest poetry. Sometimes it reads like an understatement. [For example,] in a subdued poem like *Erosion: Transkei*...the feeling is one of deep sadness rather than of outrage, of mourning rather than protest.

Beier then compared Brutus's writing to that of two other Mbari poets, Okigbo and Clark, and found Brutus

> more down to earth, closer to pressing everyday reality. He cannot indulge in purely personal poetry, he cannot afford the luxuries of mythmaking, of polished verse or extravagant imagery. He is never allowed to forget the context in which he writes, and as we leaf through his poetry we will encounter the imagery of the apartheid state on every page, regardless of the theme of his poem...
>
> Though his powerful lines convey a grim sense of reality...all...is said calmly, quietly, without bitterness. Not even the white oppressors come in for hatred, in fact they are mentioned only once, and then with a mixture of pity and contempt: "these obscene albinos."

Beier concluded by saying:

> Dennis Brutus' language and themes are almost prosy. But there is a maturity of feeling and above all a precision of phrase, that lifts this verse far above the common protest cry coming from South Africa. This simple precision of language produces almost a kind of transfiguration. And this is possible through the poet's quiet fortitude that pervades all.

I have quoted Beier at length because his comments are typical of the initial critical reaction to *Sirens Knuckles Boots*. He begins with some biographical information on Brutus, points out what kind of protest poetry is usually expected from black and colored South African writers, and then tells how Brutus defeats expectations by speaking in a refreshingly different tone of voice. There are certain assumptions implicit in this approach: (A) that nonwhite South Africans, particularly political activists, will write protest poetry; (B) that such poetry will be either "full of self-pity" or strident (or possibly both); and (C) that a nonwhite South African poet who displays "quiet fortitude" by speaking "calmly, quietly, without bitterness" in a "restrained," "disciplined," "muted" voice deserves to be heard because he sounds so unlike the tiresome hordes of "spineless," screaming protesters. One of Beier's concluding statements sums up this critical attitude: "there is a maturity of feeling and above all a *precision* of phrase, that lifts this verse far above the common protest cry coming from South Africa." In other words, Brutus is adult and controlled where others are wild and childish. He is a rare *classic* poet contributing a measure of order to an undisciplined *romantic* tradition of verse.

Critics who discuss poetry (or virtually any other form of literary expression) are apt to divide their attention in unequal proportions between three components of a work of art: the matter, the manner, and the man who created it. In the commentary on South African poetry, particularly the poetry of Brutus, there has been a tendency for critics to allow their attitudes toward the matter and the man to condition their attitudes toward the manner in which the man has articulated the matter. Beier, for instance, found it remarkable and praiseworthy that Brutus, a colored South African exploring the unavoidable themes of race prejudice, apartheid and suppression in his homeland, should adopt a subdued, almost understated tone in dealing with such explosive political issues. Beier apparently expected a noisier reaction, especially from someone who was known to be at odds with his society, and his respect for Brutus as a poet seems to have been augmented considerably by his respect for Brutus as a peaceful protester. Given oppression in South Africa as the matter and Brutus, an oppressed South African, as the man, Beier found the civilized manner of the poetry truly admirable.

Other critics coming to *Sirens Knuckles Boots* with different preconceptions about the matter or the man might evaluate the manner of this poetry very differently. Indeed, J.P. Clark's famous blast at Brutus is an excellent case in point. Speaking on "Themes of African Poetry of English Expression" at an International Meeting of Poets in Berlin in September 1964,[4] Clark dismissed Brutus's poetry in these memorable terms:

> Poetry here is servant to politics. Something of the troubadour that he proclaims himself to be, Brutus cuts a tough figure of great bravura, with quite a brutal Elizabethan hold on words, and a strong smell for all the right sentiments to stir the would-be crusader safe in his liberal seat somewhere in Europe and America. Reading the work of Dennis Brutus, much of it re-modelled rhetoric, one comes back to that old excuse by Mphahlele that certain situations like those in South Africa really are too paralysing for words. Perhaps—for what does one do to a dog holding up a mauled paw? A child in a fit of convulsion? Dennis Brutus in his book is a man battering his head against the bars of a cage in which he and his kind are undoubtedly held down by a devilish gaoler. The sight is terrible enough, but one gets the feeling sometimes, a wicked one no doubt, that a little less shouting and more silence and mime might not only make for manly dignity but also command attempts at rescue and action. That is the ram's one lesson to man when trussed up by man. In this way, what is truly tragic will not become mere melodrama—overdrawn, posturing, and tear-jerking.

Notice that Clark shares Beier's abhorrence of the oppressive South African political environment—the matter of much of Brutus's verse; he recognizes that Brutus "and his kind are undoubtedly held down by a devilish gaoler." But Clark's attitude toward the man who has produced this verse is far more sceptical and uncharitable than Beier's. By stating that Brutus is "something of the troubadour he proclaims himself to be" and a poet who "cuts a tough figure of great bravura" and has "a strong smell for all the right sentiments to stir the would-be crusader safe in his liberal seat somewhere in Europe and America," Clark manages to suggest that Brutus's persona is a mere facade or mask worn self-consciously and somewhat cynically for an explicitly political purpose; "a little less shouting," "more silence and mime," and an avoidance of futile masochism ("battering his head against the bars of a cage") "might not only make for manly dignity but also command attempts at rescue and action." A different poetic strategy would also prevent the truly tragic from deteriorating into "mere melodrama—overdrawn, posturing, and tearjerking." Clark thus recommends that Brutus, a clever artificer, change the manner of his art for the sake of his politics. If he wants to win something more than sympathy, he should stop his childish convulsions, stop holding up his mauled paw.

When one critic praises a poet for his fortitude, calmness, restraint, control and precision while another condemns him for his undignified lapses into frenzied melodrama, raucous shouting and other insincere, tear-jerking theatrics, then something must be wrong with someone's critical perceptions. How else can two critics arrive at such diametrically opposed opinions about the same corpus of poetry? One can feebly try to explain it away as merely a difference in taste: "De gustibus non est disputandum" (There is no accounting for tastes.). But if we accept what Alexander Pope noted long ago—that "All seems infected that th' infected spy,/As all looks yellow to the jaundic'd eye"[5] —then what a kaleidoscope of colors is possible when literary critics suffer from a variety of incurable perceptual disorders! Brutus's poetry may well appear yellow, red, blue, black or white, depending on the idiosyncratic squint of the individual viewer. This doesn't seem fair to the poet, who may have been trying to achieve subtler shades of meaning or to present his ideas in complex, ambiguous technicolor.

What blinds many of Brutus's critics is a set of rigid preconceptions about South Africa and about Brutus himself. The matter and the man are seen in a particular political relationship, and the poems that derive from this relationship are therefore expected to tilt in certain directions. When they do, thereby confirming the reader's ingrained or acquired habits of thought, the reader usually nods in approval. When they do not, or when they seem to take totally different positions, the reader may feel betrayed and lash out at Brutus for failing to live up to the kind of commitment demanded of an oppressed person, a prisoner or a political exile.

Pol Ndu, for instance, believes that

> The South African black or coloured man who has the opportunity should shriek, even turn militant and use all available machinations to undermine the invidious regime. In a barbarian society, only the laws of the jungle hold.[6]

For Ndu, therefore, Brutus's poetry sometimes seems too mild and dispassionate, too timid and nonrevolutionary. Ndu admits that Brutus at his best is capable of achieving a fine blend of passion and poetry, particularly when dealing with themes arising from "some loss, some desire, some feeling or even the pain of the confrontation of the abominable regime." When speaking "from the labyrinths of his fear, his anger, the wells of his thirst," he can write verse as superb as that of Sylvia Plath, who "succeeded in crystalizing in concrete terms all her fury, hatred and love." But when he mounts a soapbox and starts mouthing political propaganda or when he writes blandly about mundane things, he loses the intensity that makes his more personal lyrics memorable.

> When the passions are not completely experienced in a poet, his poetry is jagged, often sentimental and intruding. That unusual

> fuse which breaks a poem into the highest orbits of the imagination and the deepest layers of feeling is absent. In the several works of Dennis Brutus, these passions have not been fully reconciled.

Ndu finds this kind of failure in the poem "Their Behavior" which he says illustrates "Brutus' anti-Marxist theory of universal bent to greed," a theory that condemns the behavior of blacks as well as whites. Such humanistic intellectualizing, though intended as profound, only serves to impede the revolution in South Africa by inhibiting the desire of blacks to fight bitterly for social change. According to Ndu, Brutus himself

> apparently wants to fight. But his fight must not be bitter. It is not a fight of life and death—for him. It is the mercenary soldier's fight: gradual, curious but most cautious.

Ndu would prefer a more passionate approach because "the South African situation needs a realistic and grim facing up, a combat."

Ndu is therefore very disappointed with Brutus's prison "letters" which he finds too full of an emasculating mood of self-pity and an almost narcissistic indulgence in tender love for his country. Brutus seems disturbingly complacent, hopeful and optimistic in these poems. Ndu remarks that

> such optimism could in fact sustain Brutus' survival, but can never sustain equity or the hope for it in South Africa...Brutus has not fully utilized the weapons or the abilities at his disposal. Since he still lives and opportunities still abound, one would expect to see him back in the fray with fresh vigor, greater resolve and very serious weapons.

Ndu feels Brutus should stop accepting things as they are and start writing with passion "of the whites' inhumanity to the blacks in South Africa." Only then will he be able to create great poetry.

Ndu's essay is a good example of what happens to literary criticism when it is subordinated to a narrow political philosophy. The only way to write about South Africa, he suggests, is to "shriek,...turn militant and use all available machinations to undermine the invidious regime." Whining, moaning or quietly contemplating one's lot simply will not suffice. The matter invariably determines the proper manner of poetry, and when the matter is South Africa, the manner has to be sharp protest. These are the laws of the jungle in this particular barbarian society, according to Ndu.

Literary criticism which focuses on the man rather than the matter is likely to be equally myopic. Bahadur Tejani, for instance, bases his appraisal of *Letters to Martha*[7] on what he knows and does not know of Brutus's life. He begins his essay by berating Heinemann for not supplying enough "meaningful and exact" biographical information on Brutus in the blurb on the back cover of the African Writers Series edition of the book. Furthermore, the few biographical facts offered about Brutus's imprisonment, banning and poetic letter writing to his sister-in-law raise more questions than they answer.

> We are perforce made to ask: Were the poems composed *in* or *out* of prison? How did Brutus or the publishers outwit the South African Government which made it criminal to write *anything* publishable. Were the poems smuggled out of the country before they saw the light of day there? Or are "letters" a strategy of form to outwit the Minister of Justice and his censor-henchmen? If so, when and where were they first written?

These are not insignificant questions, since "the time and specially the circumstances under which Brutus wrote would color our judgement; would inform our assessment of future products from South African 'revolutionaries.'" Tejani cannot understand why this and other "important political information has been withheld or omitted," when both the poet and the publisher have been so scrupulous in providing such details as precisely when, where, for whom and on what kind of paper certain of the poems were written. Tejani also complains about the unchronological ordering of the poems in the book, for this too makes the reader's task more difficult than it should be:

> No continuity of moods, places, situations, or time, can be felt in such an arrangement. The publishers having gone all the way with Brutus's wavering mind have created a waywardness for themselves which is rare. It allows the reader to interpret the poems in any way he likes, despite the carefully contrived facade of places, towns, and dates.

Having established that it is impossible to adequately appraise Brutus's poetry with such a paucity of biographical information and such a "hotchpotch of chronology," Tejani goes on to attempt the impossible—a biographical analysis of Brutus's work. He begins by comparing Brutus's prison poetry with the poetry of Dag Hammarskjöld ("who like Brutus fought for freedom at the international level") and the prison prose of Arthur Koestler and Kenneth Kaunda. Unlike these others who were able to maintain their convictions and courageously pursue their goals in times of adversity, Brutus in his prison poems displays "no reserves of energy, no courage of beliefs from deep within, no conflict, no fortitude to buoy him against the hostile environment." Furthermore,

> Brutus' strength in dealing with experience is uncertain. The most interesting contact of prison life is homosexuality. By its very nature the sexual deviation illumines so much of what goes on underneath the facade of discipline. This the poet deals with tepidly and with veiled horror:
>
> > Perhaps most terrible are those who beg for it,
> > who beg for sexual assault.
>
> The strikingly prosaic arrangement, the allusion to "it" and the repetition of "who beg" shows a clear uncertainty, inability to face the point, in dealing with homosexuals. He is trying for emphasis,

> reassurance and self-conviction, but we feel this to be a result of the fear of becoming one of the perverted he describes.

Having thus discovered sufficient evidence in the poetry to warrant labelling Brutus a weak-willed captive and latent homosexual, Tejani proceeds to examine the "acutely prosaic arrangement of his verse," the questionable repetitions, the lack of compression and freshness—all of which can be attributed to Brutus's debilitating preoccupation with himself and "his continuous attempt to justify his own rationale" in prison.

The root of his problem, however, lies much deeper. Indeed, it is embedded in the very protoplasm of his genes. To quote Tejani:

> Finally...let me point to the fact emerging out of his poetry that weakens the foundation of Brutus's verse. The poet's special designation "Coloured" has important implications in the South African situation. By such an intermediary arrangement a man may belong in his own mind, to two races at once—"black" and "white," or to neither. But never to the third one, the "human" race, that which is his own...
>
> Brutus...is not free from the cruel irony imposed by his racist government. He is unable to choose between the "human" truths, of justice and freedom, and the "racial" truths, which are [those of] continuous comparison and equivocation based on class and culture. There is besides a sense of underlying religiousness in his poetry which makes him suspect. Indeed the simplicity and earnestness of tone is religious. Whereas elsewhere this may be a positive or neutral quality, it is purely negative in South Africa—of the seventies. There is no greater deterrent to protest against outrageous tyranny than a religion of love...
>
> Temperamentally Brutus is unsuitable to take on the sophisticated might of the South African Government. This unsuitability leads to simplistic conclusions of hope without struggle. Brutus, the mixed-up mulatto and simple-minded religious freak, is therefore a failure both as a poet and as a revolutionary.

Tejani's amateur psychologizing is typical of biographical criticism at its worst. Seeking to explain certain tendencies in Brutus's poetry by attempting to explore the unplumbed depths of his psyche, Tejani descends into a bottomless pit of pure speculation. He feels that Brutus has not responded adequately to the stimulus of prison, and he blames what he regards as failures of craft on what he imagines as deficiencies of personality. There is no way any poet can win the approval of an undisciplined head shrinker such as Tejani unless he happens to write the kind of poetry or live the kind of life that the critic is predisposed to regard as healthy and useful. Different biographical facts might sway a biographical critic to place a different evaluation on a poet's work.

And, of course, the same biographical facts may strike different biographical critics in different ways. One can detect in some of the criticism of Brutus's poetry a tendency toward hero-worship, toward enthusiastic acceptance of the poetry because it has been written by a man the critic admires. Such criticism is often prefaced by an account of the hardships and brutality Brutus had to face in South Africa as well as by a record of his achievements after going into exile. Since Brutus has not had a dull life, this interesting biographical data can easily win him friends and supporters. As Tejani puts it:

> Can anyone who has known the modern interactions between the South African Government and the Africans, and the power of gold and anti-communism with which South Africa baits the great powers, fail to sympathize with this summary of Brutus's career? Singularly responsible for South Africa's Olympic expulsion, arrested in 1963, escaped, handed over to the South African Security Police by the Portuguese, shot in the back while trying again to escape, a teacher for fourteen years, married with eight children, brother in prison, poems written for sister-in-law for her "grief, loss and care" in the poet's own words; the situation is classic.

Indeed, the situation is so classic that it leads Tejani to expect too much; he says, "We are justified in turning to the verse with heightened expectation of another Doctor Zhivago confronting us with the destiny of Man under totalitarianism and more, racialism." Naturally, Tejani feels disappointed when his great expectations are not fulfilled.

But for other critics, Brutus's impressive vita may actually lower rather than heighten literary expectations. Their feeling might be akin to that experienced by readers of newsmagazines who discover that famous public figures such as Eugene McCarthy, Spiro Agnew, Muhammad Ali and Jimmy Carter dabble in the arts of poetry and fiction. One may be interested in reading a sample of their work but one does not expect such men of affairs to achieve a very high level of literary accomplishment. If they display a modicum of talent, they may win more applause for their creative efforts than they really merit.

This is not to say that Brutus has been praised for the wrong reasons. He has many genuine admirers who are far more interested in his poetry than in his politics or personal life. Yet even some of these critics, rigorous though they may attempt to be in their evaluation of his work, occasionally fall into the trap of sympathizing with the poet-protester, the poet-prisoner or the poet-politician. For instance, Romanus Egudu, in an otherwise fairly objective assessment of his poetry, offers this rather startling explanation of why "Brutus can be prosaic and allow poetry to escape him at times" in *Letters to Martha*.[8]

> It can be argued in his favour that the weight of sorrow was so heavy upon his heart that he became unsettled mentally and could not pay necessary attention to his art. The pressure of the matter was too oppressive for the manner of its expression to be attended to. And like Christ, Brutus could justly proclaim: the thought of your (prisoners') plight has eaten up my heart!

The image of Brutus as a mentally unbalanced Christ-figure is biographical speculation pushed to an unctuous extreme. The obvious implication is that our long-suffering hero is capable of writing bad verse only when he is momentarily insane. If this is true, a less sympathetic critic playing devil's advocate might respond by arguing that there is more than ample evidence in *Letters to Martha* and his later verse to warrant having Brutus committed to an asylum!

What we learn from these comments by Egudu, Tejani, Ndu, Clark, Beier and others is that biographical criticism and sociological criticism are highly subjective and can carry us only so far into interpretation of a poet's work. Indeed, usually they attempt to carry us too far and the result is a highly questionable exegesis. Lewis Nkosi tried to warn us long ago that "We cannot really judge how good the poet Dennis Brutus is by simply counting the number of guns he has carried to the revolutionary front."[9] Assumptions—positive or negative—about the man or about the battle he is fighting should not influence our judgement of his poetry. It is the manner of that poetry rather than the matter or the man which should be the primary concern of critics.

However, this is not to argue that the man and the matter are unimportant or illegitimate critical concerns. Obviously, it may help a critic to know the opinion an author holds on a subject he chooses to write about. Certain topics—for instance, prison, revolution, war, death—will carry such heavy emotional freight that a responsible critic will be unable to ignore their inherent connotative value. Yet a poem about prison, revolution, war or death will not necessarily be a good poem simply because the topic is sensitive and the poet's heart is in the right place. The words chosen to deal with that topic must do all the work, must effectively convey the idea or emotion, must force the reader to respond. Poetry by its very nature is a verbal art and therefore cannot be properly evaluated by criteria which shift the center of attention to something other than the words themselves. T.S. Eliot once remarked that "the poet has, not a 'personality' to express, but a particular medium, which is only a medium and not a personality."[10] We must judge every poet according to how well he expresses his medium rather than how well he expresses his personality or his politics.

Critics who attempt to deal with the poetry of Dennis Brutus are therefore confronted with a formidable challenge to their analytical abilities. They must learn to keep their eye on the art without being distracted by the character of the artist or his environment. A few critics—Anthony Astrachan, Paul Theroux, Daniel Abasiekong, Edwin Thumboo—have already risen to the challenge with some degree of success, but no one has yet been able to distance himself sufficiently from the matter or the man behind the poetry.[11]

Perhaps this is the central problem with Brutus's poetry. It invites intimacy and encourages, anticipates—indeed, sometimes even demands—the concurrence of the reader in the opinions of the writer. Evil and good are defined in terms and symbols with which the reader is assumed or expected to agree. The liberal critic, aware of the specific sociopolitical circumstances that have prompted the poetry and eager to demonstrate solidarity with the poet, therefore expends much of his energy and ink denouncing apartheid and expressing sympathy for nonwhite South Africans in general and Brutus in particular. Such critics ordinarily arrive at a favorable assessment of the poetry. The critics who arrive at unfavorable assessments—Clark, Ndu and Tejani, for example—are most often those who cannot agree with Brutus's political views, who believe that South African poetry should arouse people to action rather than merely elicit their sympathy, who dismiss as ineffectual and counterrevolutionary any maudlin display of the softer emotions. These "more-militant-than-thou" commissars of culture usually pay little attention to matters of form, preferring to comment on matters of ideology, commitment and artistic strategy.

The critic who wishes to achieve a more balanced view of Brutus's poetry than any that have been offered so far will have to strive for the kind of objective detachment from both the man and the matter that will enable him to appraise the manner of the poetry with unfettered insight and critical integrity. Only then will Brutus be accorded the serious attention he deserves—not as a suffering South African, not as a political prisoner, not as an exiled intellectual, not as a revolutionary, but as a poet.

NOTES

1. *Sirens Knuckles Boots* (Ibadan: Mbari, 1963).

2. *Letters to Martha and Other Poems from a South African Prison* (London: Heinemann, 1968); *Poems from Algiers* (Austin: African and Afro-American Research Institute, University of Texas, 1970); (under pseudonym John Bruin) *Thoughts Abroad* (Del Valle, Texas: Troubadour Press, 1970); *A Simple Lust* (London: Heinemann, 1973); *China Poems* (Austin: African and Afro-American, Studies and Research Center, University of Texas, 1975); *Strains* (Austin: Troubadour Press, 1975); *Stubborn Hope* (Washington DC: Three Continents Press; London: Heinemann, 1978); *Salutes and Censures* (Enugu, Nigeria: Fourth Dimension, 1984); *Airs and Tributes* (Camden, NJ: Whirlwind Press, 1989); *Still the Sirens* (Santa Fe, NM: Pennywhistle Press, 1993).

3. *Conference of African Writers of English Expression* (Kampala: Department of Extra-Mural Studies, Makerere University, [1972]), pp. MAK/II(4), 5-7; *Black Orpheus*, 12 (n.d.), 49-50.

4. Originally printed as "Poetry in Africa Today," *Transition*, 18 (1965), 23; reprinted as "Themes of African Poetry of English Expression" in Clark's *The Example of Shakespeare* (London: Longman, 1970), p. 50. It was this comment that prompted Wole Soyinka to remark at another conference that

> I do not, alas, possess the superior complacency of a fellow writer from Africa who uttered sentiments more or less in the following words: "One is tempted to ask," he says, "what is the South African writer doing for himself? A little less talking and protest and a bit more action, especially from the so-called exiles, might be more to the point..." etc. I regret very much that I have not the exact quotation here, for it is the kind of remark which proves very clearly that the easiest solution to any problem is to maintain complete ignorance of it.

See Soyinka's "The Writer in a Modern Africa State," *Transition*, 31 (1967), 11, and reprinted in *The Writer in Modern Africa*, ed. Per Wästberg (Uppsala: Scandinavian Institute of African Studies, 1968), p. 14.

5. "An Essay on Criticism," *The Poems of Alexander Pope*, I (London: Dent, 1961), II. 558-59.

6. Pol Ndu, "Passion and Poetry in the Works of Dennis Brutus," *Black Academy Review*, 2, 1/2 (1971), 41-54; reprinted in *Modern Black Literature*, ed. S. Okechukwu Mezu (Buffalo, N. Y.: Black Academy Press, 1971), pp. 41-54.

7. Bahadur Tejani, "Can the Prisoner Make a Poet? A Critical Discussion of *Letters to Martha* by Dennis Brutus," *African Literature Today*, 6 (1973), 130-44; a slightly different version of this essay entitled "The Prison Poems of Dennis Brutus" appears in *Standpoints on African Literature*, ed. Chris L. Wanjala (Nairobi, Kampala, Dar es Salaam: East African Literature Bureau, 1973), pp. 323-43. Quotations have been selected from whichever version read best. Tejani's readings of several of Brutus's poems have been strongly challenged by M. J. Salt, "On the Business of Literary Criticism: With Special Reference to Bahadur Tejani's 'Can the Prisoner Make a Poet?'" *African Literature Today*, 7 (1975), 128-41.

8. "Pictures of Pain: The Poetry of Dennis Brutus," paper presented at the inaugural conference of the African Literature Association held in Austin, Texas, March 19-22, 1975. This essay appeared in *Aspects of South African Literature*, ed. Christopher Heywood (London: Heinemann; New York: Africana, 1976).

9. "Individualism and Social Commitment," in Wästberg, p. 47.

10. *The Sacred Wood* (3rd ed. London: Methuen 1932), p. 56.

11. Anthony M. Astrachan, "Creative Writing," *Nigeria Magazine*, 79 (1963), 290-92; Paul Theroux, "Voices out of the Skull: A Study of Six African Poets," *Black Orpheus*, 20 (1966), 41-58, and reprinted in *Introduction to African Literature*, ed. Ulli Beier (Evanston: Northwestern University Press, 1967), pp. 110-31; Daniel Abasiekong, "Poetry Pure and Applied: Rabearivelo and Brutus," *Transition*, 23 (1965), 45-48; Edwin Thmboo, "Dennis Brutus: Apartheid and the Troubadour," *Joliso*, 2, 2 (1974), 31-46. John Povey has also written two brief essays on Brutus: "Simply to Stand," *Journal of the New African Literature and the Arts*, 3 (1967), 95-100, and "Dennis Brutus: Poetry and Politics," *Ba Shiru*, 4, 2 (1973), 12-15.

Dialectical Development in the Poetry of Dennis Brutus

There have been four distinct phases in Dennis Brutus's poetic development, each marked by formal and thematic shifts which tend not only to reflect his changing preoccupations and professional concerns but also to document profound transformations in his conception of the nature and function of poetry. Each new phase has grown out of a personal experience which has made him question his previous attitudes toward verbal art and seek a more satisfying outlet for his energies of articulation. As a consequence, his progress as a poet cannot be charted as a straight line moving up, down or forever forward on a monotonous horizontal plane; rather, it must be visualized as a series of reversals or turnabouts, each fresh impulse moving in a direction counter to its antecedent until an entirely new lyrical idiom is achieved. To put it in ontogenetic terms, Brutus's evolution as a poet has been not linear but dialectical. Instead of growing by extending himself further and further along a single axis, he has zigzagged.

The four poles around which Brutus's art has turned may be termed Complexity, Simplicity, Balance and Economy, the latter being an extreme form of Simplicity. These poles roughly correspond to the Hegelian triad—Thesis, Antithesis, Synthesis—with Synthesis, a balance between Thesis and Antithesis, becoming a new Thesis and generating its own Antithesis. To translate these abstractions into an appropriate geometrical configuration, one could represent Brutus's career as follows:

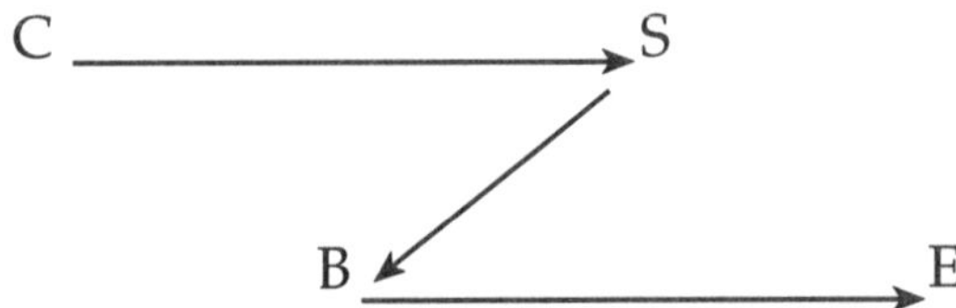

Having postulated this theorem of dialectical development, let us now go on to examine the proof upon which it rests.

Brutus's first book of poems, *Sirens Knuckles Boots* (1963), contained a variety of lyric forms invested with many of the standard poetic conventions. There were neatly demarcated stanzas, end-rhymes, assonance, alliteration, bookish allusions, carefully balanced contrasts, paradoxes, skillful reiterations and refrains that enlarged rather than merely repeated an idea, well-reasoned arguments couched in logically connected images, and utterances so rich in symbolic suggestiveness that they spoke at several levels of significance simultaneously. There were no loose ends in this poetry, no wasted words, no compromises with the reader's dull-wittedness. This was highbrow poetry—tight, mannered, formal and sometimes formidably difficult. Schooled in Shakespeare, Donne, Browning, Hopkins, Eliot and other classic English poets of exceptional intellect, Brutus attempted to write poems which would challenge the mind, poems sufficiently subtle and intricate to interest any well-educated lover of poetry. It was during this period that he wrote nearly all of his most complex verse.

Brutus's greatest imaginative achievement in *Sirens Knuckles Boots* was the creation of an ambiguous idiom which allowed him to make both a political and an erotic statement in the same breath. Some of his poems can be read superficially as straightforward love lyrics but lurking just beneath the surface is a political undercurrent which turns the passion into militant protest. The loved one is not only a particular woman but also the poet-speaker's homeland, and the torments he experiences when contemplating her spectacular beauty, tenderness and ability to endure great suffering spur him on to bolder efforts on her behalf, efforts by which he can express the intensity of his love for her. A good example of this kind of double-breasted love lyric is "Erosion: Transkei," where the word "Eros" embedded in "Erosion" is a deliberate pun.

> Under green drapes the scars scream,
> red wounds wail soundlessly,
> beg for assuaging, satiation;
> warm life dribbles seawards with the streams.
>
> Dear my land, open for my possessing,
> ravaged and dumbly submissive to our will,
> in curves and uplands my sensual delight
> mounts, and mixed with fury is amassing
>
> torrents tumescent with love and pain.
> Deep-dark and rich, with deceptive calmness
> time and landscape flow to new horizons—
> in anguished impatience await the quickening rains.[1]

In addition to the *double-entendre* that informs this entire poem, it is worth noting the formal structure the poetic statement takes. Three four-line stanzas slant-rhyming ABCA (scream/streams; possessing/amassing; pain/rains) are peppered with assonance and alliteration (e.g., "scars scream," "wounds wail," "assuaging, satiation," and the deft intermingling of long *a* and short *i* sounds in the last rhythmic line: "in anguished impatience await the quickening rains"). The poem opens with a description of tormented deprivation as old and new injuries (scars, red wounds) cry out for comfort and fulfillment. The cries of the ravaged loved one are soundless so there is a "deceptive calmness" to her plea. The poet-speaker responds with his own plea, asking her to submit to his painful and furiously mounting love. Their union promises to bring relief by producing new life, but immediate consummation of their desires is not achieved. The poem ends as it began, with the loved one, the land, waiting in agony and impatience for satisfying change. As in many other poems in *Sirens Knuckles Boots*, the poetic argument is rounded off by a reassertion of the initial idea.

The political thrust of this poem is made more explicit by the title which identifies the despoiled landscape as the Transkei, the area of the Republic of South Africa which was designated as the first Bantustan, or Bantu homeland. The erosion of the Transkei is not only a geological reality but also clear evidence of social injustice and political oppression. But such erosion, such pain, such impatience for revolutionary change is not confined to only one area of Southern Africa. The Transkei also functions as a metaphor for all Bantustans and ghettos created by apartheid and other institutionalized forms of racial discrimination. The message thus has universal as well as local reverberations.

"Erosion: Transkei" is a fairly uncomplicated multi-levelled lyric compared with such poems as "A troubadour, I traverse all my land" and "So for the moment, Sweet, is peace," upon which Brutus has commented extensively.[2] In the troubadour poem, for instance, there are lines in which he attempted to make a single image yield at least three different meanings simultaneously. The word "Sweet" in "So, for the moment, Sweet, is peace" also had numerous special connotations for him. Indeed, it would be very difficult for even the most astute student of literary ambiguity to decipher the full range of significance that such words and images were meant to carry without consulting the gloss that Brutus has provided in discussions of these poems. Some of the symbolism is private, cryptic and therefore impenetrable to anyone but the poet himself. Such poetry requires translation for the average reader.

It was while Dennis Brutus was in prison between 1964 and 1965 that he decided to stop writing this kind of super-cerebral poetry. The five months he spent in solitary confinement caused him to reexamine his verse and his attitudes toward creative self-expression. The more he looked at his poetry during this period of forced isolation, the more "horrified" he became, until finally he decided that if he were ever to write again, he would write very differently:

> The first thing I decided about my future poetry was that there must be no ornament, absolutely none. And the second thing I decided was you oughtn't to write for people who read poetry, not even students. You ought to write for the ordinary person: for the man who drives a bus, or the man who carries the baggage at the airport, and the woman who cleans the ashtrays in the restaurant. If you can write poetry which makes sense to those people, then there is some justification for writing poetry. Otherwise you have no business writing.
>
> And therefore, there should be no ornament because ornament gets in the way. It becomes too fancy-schmancy; it becomes overelaborate. It is, in a way, a kind of pride, a self-display, a glorying in the intellect for its own sake, which is contemptible . . .
>
> So I said, "You will have to set the thing down. You will 'tell it like it is,' but you will let the word do its work in the mind of the reader. And you will write poetry that a man who drives a bus along the street can quote, if he feels like quoting." Very ambitious indeed.
>
> But this is based on the idea that all people are poets. Some are just ashamed to let it be known, and some are shy to try, and some write but don't have the guts to show it to others. But we all are poets because we all have the same kind of response to beauty. We may define beauty differently, but we all do respond to it.
>
> So this was the assumption: don't dress it up; you will just hand it over, and it will do its own work.[3]

The first poems he wrote after making this resolution were collected in *Letters to Martha and Other Poems from a South African Prison* (1968). The change in idiom was immediately apparent. The diction was far simpler; rigid poetic devices such as end-rhyme, metrical regularity and symmetrical stanza structure had been all but abandoned; conceits, tortuously logical paradoxes, and tantalizingly ambiguous image-clusters could no longer be found; ornament—ornament of virtually every kind—had vanished almost entirely. The result was a flat, conversational mode of poetry which surprised and in some cases alarmed readers who had admired the technical complexity of the poems in his first volume and had expected more of the same in his second. Now, instead of saying three things at once, Brutus was saying one thing at a time and saying it very directly. He was creating a poetry of plain statement, a poetry which bus drivers, porters and cleaning women could understand and presumably appreciate.

One example of this new idiom may suffice; describing life in prison, he wrote in the tenth "letter" to his sister-in-law Martha:

> It is not all terror
> and deprivation,
> you know;
>
> one comes to welcome the closer contact
> and understanding one achieves
> with one's fellow-men
> fellows, compeers;
>
> and the discipline does much to force
> a shape and pattern on one's daily life
> as well as on the days
>
> and honest toil
> offers some redeeming hours
> for the wasted years;
>
> so there are times
> when the mind is bright and restful
> though alive:
> rather like the full calm morning sea.[4]

Until the last line, there is not even an image in this poem. Moreover, when "the full calm morning sea" is introduced, it enters the poem as a simile, not as a metaphor or symbol with wider connotative value. Like all the other ideas in the poem, it is there for a specific purpose and it has only one meaning. This is Brutus at his simplest.

Not every poem in *Letters to Martha* is this stark, of course. There are some, such as "Longing" (dated August 1960) and

"Abolish laughter first, I say" (dated "Mid fifties"), which actually derive from the earlier *Sirens* period and manifest many of the complexities characteristic of Brutus's early work. Also, there are several which are not quite as simple as they seem—the "Colesberg" poem, for example, the subtleties of which Brutus has explicated at some length.[5]

Moreover, one finds certain of the older tendencies—the well-rounded statement, the learned allusion or quotation, the harmonious imagery—resurfacing in several poems and giving an orderly appearance to even the freest-flowing lines. In other words, there is evidence of continuity as well as change as Brutus shifts from complex to simple registers of poetic expression. The transformation is sudden and obvious but not absolute.

In July 1966, a year after being released from prison, Brutus left South Africa on an "exit permit," a permit which did not allow him to reenter his homeland. His life in exile began with four years of anti-apartheid work in London and has continued since September 1970 in the United States, where he has been teaching as Professor of English at Northwestern University, in the 1974-75 academic year as Visiting Professor of English and Ethnic Studies at the University of Texas at Austin, and more recently as Chairman of Africana Studies at the University of Pittsburgh. During these years his poetry has undergone two modifications, first a minor modulation to a position earlier described as Balance, then a major shift to what could be called extreme Economy. Again, though these two successive changes are observable in much of what he has written since going into exile, one occasionally finds new poems which could be placed in the earlier categories of Complexity or Simplicity. In other words, Brutus retains the capacity to express himself in his earlier poetic modes even while consciously attempting to define a new style. Whereas certain of the poems he has composed in exile can be viewed as throwbacks or lapses into a former habit of articulation, the fresh impulses, the newer tendencies are dominant in most of what he has written since July 1966.

The two major thematic preoccupations in Brutus's early exile poetry are (1) his awareness of the personal freedom and mobility he has gained while others remain confined and suffering in South Africa, and (2) his recognition of what he has lost in leaving the homeland he dearly loves and travelling restlessly about the world in quest of compelling but sometimes elusive goals. Much of this poetry could be characterized as both nostalgic and plaintive—the unhappy recollections and reflections of a homesick poet. Examples can be taken from *Poems from Algiers* (1970) which was written while Brutus was attending the First Pan-African Cultural Festival in Algiers in 1969, *Thoughts Abroad* (1970) which was written piecemeal in various cities throughout the world and published under a pseudonym so it could be sold and circulated in South Africa, and Part III of *A Simple Lust* (1973) which includes some American and English poems as well as the verse published in the two preceding collections.

Perhaps a good place to begin would be with one of the first London poems in *A Simple Lust*:

> I walk in the English quicksilver dusk
> and spread my hands to the soft spring rain
> and see the streetlights gild the flowering trees
> and the late light breaking through patches of broken cloud
> and I think of the Island's desolate dusks
> and the swish of the Island's haunting rain
> and the desperate frenzy straining our prisoned breasts:
> and the men who are still there crouching now
> in the grey cells, on the grey floors, stubborn and bowed.[6]

The painful recollection of Robben Island, the contrast between freedom and confinement, the manifold sensory perceptions—all these are typical of Brutus's poetry in exile, but even more noteworthy is the full-bodied texture of the poem. Brutus is no longer writing unornamented verse. The diction is simple, the form irregular, the line length flexible instead of fixed, but there are also traces of alliteration, slanted end-rhymes (dusk/dusks/breasts; rain/rains; cloud/now/bowed), and deliberate parallelism in the seven lines beginning with the word "and." Moreover, the rhetorical structure of the poetic statement is carefully balanced to make an effective contrast. The silver and gold ambience of an English dusk is off-set by the desolate greyness of South African prison cells. England's "soft spring rain" is placed in opposition to Robben Island's "haunting rain." The poet-speaker walks freely and spreads his hands expansively while the prisoners crouch "stubborn and bowed." The poem is not a bald string of abstract nouns and verbs stretched out into a prosaic statement but rather a succession of graphic, sentient perceptions which turn poignant when juxtaposed. Because of its rich texture, because it is obviously well-wrought without being highly mannered or ambiguous, this poem must be placed somewhere between the polar extremes of Complexity and Simplicity toward which Brutus had gravitated previously. It is a middle-of-the-road poem, neither excessively plain nor unusually fancy. It belongs to the period of Balance (or Synthesis) in Brutus's poetry.

Perhaps another example will be helpful here, this time a poem about poetry itself:

> Sometimes a mesh of ideas
> webs the entranced mind,
> the assenting delighted mental eye;
> and sometimes the thrust and clash
> of forged and metalled words
> makes musical clangour in the brain;
> and sometimes a nude and simple word
> standing unlit or unadorned
> may plead mutely in cold or dark
> for an answering warmth, an enlightening sympathy;
> state the bare fact and let it sing.[7]

The poetic statement, trisected into meticulously counterpoised clauses which onomatopoetically render three of the stylistic options available to any user of language, is artful without being enigmatic. Though the poem yields its meaning easily and with seemingly effortless grace, it is actually more complicated than it appears, depending for its effect on a calculated orchestration of syntax, image and sound toward the trim finality of the last line: "state the bare fact and let it sing." Such singing is not done effectively without a good score. In the best of Brutus's balanced poetry, his compositional scoring is surreptitious, his art almost invisible.

Brutus might have remained a well-balanced poet longer had he not been invited to the Peoples' Republic of China in the summer of 1973 to represent the South African Table Tennis Board and the South African Non-Racial Olympic Committee at a Friendship Invitational Table Tennis Tournament in which eighty-six countries from Africa, Asia and Latin America participated. Shortly before taking the trip he discovered Mao Tse-tung's poetry in a new translation by Willis Barnstone and Ko Ching-Po. Extremely impressed with Mao's classic economy as a poet, he began to experiment with Chinese modes of poetic expression, attempting to capture in his own verse in English the Spartan laconism of what he had read. In a note to his *China Poems* (1975) Brutus explains his intention:

> Even before my trip I had begun to work towards more economical verse. My exposure to *haikus* and their even tighter Chinese ancestors, the *chueh chu*, impelled me further. The trick is to say little (the nearer to nothing, the better) and to suggest much—as much as possible. The weight of meaning hovers around the words (which should be as flat as possible) or is brought by the reader/ hearer. Non-emotive, near-neutral sounds should generate unlimited resonances in the mind; the delight is in the tight-rope balance between nothing and everything possible; between saying very little and implying a great deal. Here are examples, from other sources, of this form.
>
> Goose-grey
> clouds
> lour

> There is an enormous gap to be traversed in the mind between softness (silliness is also suggested) of "goose-grey" and the thunderous menace of "lour" presaging a storm.
>
> Exile:
> schizophrenia:
> suicide
>
> Consider the terror of the journey to be made in the mind from exile to the declension of suicide.[8]

The verse in Brutus's *China Poems* is economical to the point of being epigrammatic. Take, for example, the following three mini-poems.

> It is to preserve
> beauty
> that we destroy.
>
> The Chinese carver
> building a new world:
> chips of ivory in his hair.
>
> At the Long Wall:
> a soldier
> holding a flower.[9]

These poems operate on the principle of paradox, of unexpected and seemingly illogical leaps of thought or image which give the impression of being self-contradictory: we destroy in order to preserve; chips of an ancient art material (ivory) play a part in building a new world; a soldier holds a flower. The tightrope balance here appears to be between sense and nonsense, between premises at variance with conclusions. The initial images briefly build up expectations and the final image knocks them down. The imagination sets out on its journey and gets ambushed at the end. It is the ability of these poems to astonish and betray us that makes them successful.

There are also several vignettes among the China poems which gain their strength from irony, the cousin of paradox. Here are two:

On the roofs
of the ruined palaces of Emperors
imperial lions snarl
at the empty air.

The tree in the Emperor's Garden
will not accept
the discipline of marble.[10]

It is easy to read political messages in these ironies, but different readers might be inclined to interpret them in different ways. For instance, the undisciplined tree in the Emperor's Garden could mean one thing to a Chinese Mainlander and something else to a Taiwanese. Explication of the image would depend entirely on one's point of view. Here is where extreme economy backfires on the economist. Or does it? Perhaps part of the strategy of generating "unlimited resonances in the mind" is to create ironies, ambiguities and contradictions which can never be completely resolved. A few well-chosen words could conceivably produce myriad tensions in the imagination. The poet would thus get maximum mental mileage with a minimum of energy. What he might lose in precision by such economy he would certainly regain in amplitude.

Not all of Brutus's China poems achieve such heady inflation, however. Several fall so utterly flat that they cannot be resuscitated. A banal observation such as

Peasants, workers
they are the strength
of the land.

never gets off the ground poetically, but it is no worse than:

Miles of corn:
it is simple:
life is simple.

which is simply too simple for words. My favorite verbal void, however, is Brutus's toast at a sixty-course banquet in the Great Hall of the People, the Chinese Parliament. It consists of but six words, one of which is repeated three times:

Good food
good wine
good friendship.[11]

To which one is tempted to add, somewhat rudely, "but not good poetry."

During his year in Austin, Brutus continued to experiment with economical poetic forms, adapting the Chinese idiom he admires to suit new subject matter and new emotions. I am not at liberty to discuss certain of these unpublished works but Brutus has consented to allow me to quote a few examples of recent tendencies in his terse verse. One of these was dashed off, I recall, shortly after we had been discussing the care and preservation of his manuscripts.

Bach's wife, they say
made curlpapers
from his manuscripts.[12]

He has written many other minipoems equally flippant in tone. These "one-liners" in two or three lines represent the lighter side of his present poetic disposition.

A more serious side is visible in poems concerned with his relationship to South Africa. He still writes homesick verse occasionally, focusing on the disquieting reminders of South Africa which intrude upon his awareness at odd moments, forcing him to contemplate his existence in exile. His six-poem "South African Sequence" in *South African Voices* sounds a familiar plaintive note, but the individual poems now tend to be shorter, pithier, more Chinese:

> Golden oaks and jacarandas
> flowering:
> exquisite images
> to wrench my heart.

Another sample:

> At night
> to put myself to sleep
> I play alphabet games
> but something reminds me of you
> and I cry out
> and am wakened.[13]

Economy remains the defining principle of these poems.

It would be misleading, however, to suggest that Brutus has given up writing longer poems entirely and has never returned to former habits of composition since visiting China. At times it is necessary for him to make an extended statement, especially when he wants to underscore a specific political point or get a personal message across to a particular individual. But even in these instances the longer poems he writes today tend to be a bit simpler and freer than those he wrote a few years ago in his balanced phase. If he periodically swings away from austere economy, he does so in the direction of extended simplicity rather than of increased complexity. To put it in Hegelian terms again, the Synthesis of his Balanced phase and his Economical phase is a new form of Simplicity—Neo-Simplicity, if you like. On the graph it could be represented thus:

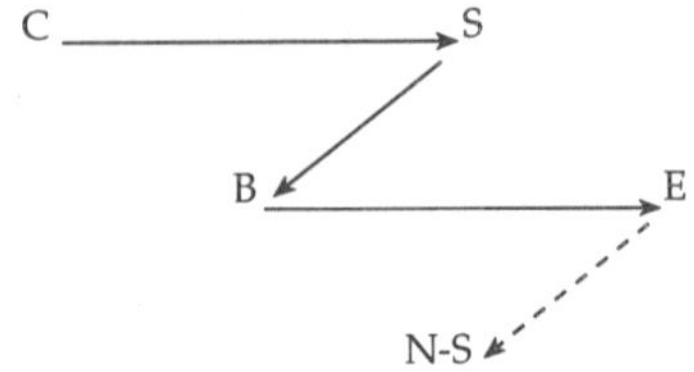

Though Brutus may not yet have swung in the direction of Neo-Simplicity emphatically enough for us to delineate it as a major tendency in his current development, it seems reasonable to assume that it may still offer him the only acceptable alternative to the taciturn Chinese modes of expression he has been favoring since the summer of 1973. If the pendulum ever swings completely away from extreme Economy, it is unlikely that it will swing all the way back to Balance or Complexity.

If we follow this dialectical progression to its logical conclusion, the next step after Neo-Simplicity—indeed the only Antithesis that would take Brutus beyond extreme Economy—would be Silence, an absolute cessation of poetic articulation. Curiously enough, Brutus appears to have anticipated moving ultimately in this direction. In a four-line poem written in February, 1975, he said:

> Music, at its highest
> strains toward silence:
> verse, when most expressive,
> seeks to be wordless.[14]

At this point criticism must become wordless too.

NOTES

1. Dennis Brutus, *A Simple Lust* (New York: Hill and Wang, 1973), p. 16. Two errors which appeared in this poem when originally published in *Sirens Knuckles Boots* (Ibadan: Mbari Publications, 1963) have been corrected in this collection of Brutus's poetry.

2. "Interview with Dennis Brutus," *Palaver: Interviews with Five African Writers in Texas*, ed. Bernth Lindfors et al. (Austin: African and Afro-American Research Institute, University of Texas, 1972), pp. 26-28, 34-36.

3. Ibid., p. 29.

4. *A Simple Lust*, pp. 60-61. The poem originally appeared in *Letters to Martha and Other Poems from a South African Prison* (London: Heinemann, 1968), p. 11.

5. *Palaver*, pp. 29-31.

6. *A Simple Lust*, p. 102.

7. Ibid., p. 136.

8. Dennis Brutus, *China Poems* (Austin: African and Afro-American Studies and Research Center, University of Texas, 1975), p. 35.

9. Ibid., pp. 18, 24, 17.

10. Ibid., pp. 10, 9..

11. Ibid., pp. 20, 21, 12.

12. Unpublished ms.

13. *South African Voices*, ed. Bernth Lindfors (Austin: African and Afro-American Studies and Research Center, University of Texas, 1975), pp. 31-32.

14. Dennis Brutus, *Strains* (Austin: Troubadour Press, 1975), p. 44.

Wole Soyinka, When Are You Coming Home?

Let me begin by stating unequivocally that I regard Wole Soyinka as one of the greatest writers Africa has produced. His work is of consistently high quality, and he appears to be so abundantly gifted as to be able to achieve without visible effort virtually any literary effect he desires. Intense creative energy bristles beneath every page he writes, charging his words with the kind of intellectual electricity that only true genius generates. A high-voltage literary dynamo, he possesses magnificent power to shock, stimulate, agitate, ignite, activate, enlighten and all the while entertain his audience. He has got what it takes to move men and set them thinking.

Yet there seems to be a calamitous short circuit somewhere in this impressive engine. Perhaps some wires are loose. Perhaps constant friction has worn away several vital points of contact. Perhaps the climate has finally taken its toll, for the rains in the tropics are known to beat down very heavily on any upright presence that does not bother to seek the cozy security of an insulated protective shelter. Soyinka, in attempting to brave the harsher elements of his society, may have blown his own fuse, for there is increasing evidence of a tragic misapplication of power, a near total blackout of illumination. More and more frequently the artist simply fails to communicate his message to the world.

In a lesser writer this would be forgivable because neither the message nor the art would be significant enough to alter our consciousness. But Soyinka is a writer who can teach us something new about human realities, about ourselves, about all mankind. He sees clearly where others only grope in darkness. He has demonstrated his acuity of vision time and time again so people are in the habit of listening when he speaks. This makes his enigmatic obfuscations seem even more perverse and irresponsible. Just as we are beginning to trust the man and take him seriously, he toys with us, spouting nonsense instead of wisdom. I don't think we can afford to go on pretending that all his obscure riddles are profound. The world is in such a mess already that it cannot tolerate much more confusion. The socially committed writer must speak to his people in a language they can understand.

Although he might deny it,[1] there can be little doubt that Wole Soyinka believes writers ought to he socially committed. At recent conferences and symposia, in articles, interviews and broadcasts, he has frequently asserted that the writer should function as the conscience of his society, should serve as "the special eye and ear, the special knowledge and response" which provides a "unique reflection on experience and events"[2] for the benefit of his people. At a conference in Stockholm he spoke of the need for the African writer to function "as the record of the mores and experience of his society *and* as the voice of vision in his own time."[3] For Soyinka the prophetic role is even more important than the documentary role; he went on at this conference to insist that

> it is about time the African writer stopped being a mere chronicler and understood also that part of his essential purpose in society is to write with a very definite vision. After that, if he prefers to retire into his cave to protect himself, then it is just fine, but he must at least begin by exposing the future in a clear and truthful exposition of the present.[4]

One could debate whether this means the writer should be didactic. In an interview recorded as early as 1962, before any of his major works had been published, Soyinka said:

> my prime duty as a playwright is to provide excellent theatre, in other words, I think that I have only one commitment to the public, and that is to my audience and that is to make sure they do not leave the theatre bored. I don't believe that I have any obligation to enlighten, to instruct, to teach: I don't possess that sense of duty or didacticism.

However, he quickly qualified this by adding "But inevitably, it is just common sense to say that one just cannot write about just nothing."[5] Soyinka's later statements show a more mature sense of social responsibility, a deep-rooted conviction that the writer who wishes to serve as seer in his society must do more than merely distract his audience from boredom; he must communicate his vision of the human condition to those who are too shortsighted or blind to see it clearly themselves. In other words, he must convey a truth, a lucid social metaphor. A seer must not only be able to see; he must also be able to transfer his vision to others.

It is in this second task that Soyinka frequently fails. As poet, playwright and prose writer, he too often offers nothing but scrambled messages, subtle verbal puzzles that scholars must labor to decode. Certainly he cannot claim to be addressing himself to the common man. The ordinary Nigerian has no hope of understanding him when he lapses into one of his mystic trances and turns on the faucet of foaming words full blast. Even intelligent Nigerian undergraduates and their professors are known to be baffled by his more delirious conundrums. One could argue, of course, that he is not writing for the masses, that he is really writing for a tiny elite, rather like Einstein whose advanced theories could be understood by only a handful of men during his lifetime. This is the kind of flattering comparison that defenders of Soyinka's cryptic private dialogues with cosmic vacuity like to make, but I would remind these apostles that there are lunatics howling in the streets of Ibadan and Lagos whose furious, empty rhetoric is every bit as colorful and meaningless as Soyinka's most inspired gibberish. Where do we draw the line between profundity and profligacy, between method and madness in the manipulation of words? Why should we be awed by sheer unintelligibility? If the prophet speaks in an incomprehensible tongue, who will listen to him? Who will learn from him? He might as well be mute.

It may be misleading to suggest that Soyinka developed this regrettable tendency towards semantic anarchy only recently. The disease appears to have set in quite early in his career. The first public evidence of it was *A Dance of the Forests*, a play commissioned and performed for the Nigerian independence celebrations of 1960 and published by Oxford University Press in 1963. Oxford brought out his full-length comedy *The Lion and the Jewel* at the same time, and it is interesting to compare these plays to see the two directions in which the young playwright was being drawn almost simultaneously. *The Lion and the Jewel* is a brilliant sex comedy in which the magnetic field of attraction and repulsion between three characters caught in an amusing African variation of the classic love triangle is presented with absolute clarity. We understand the characters and the situation perfectly, yet Soyinka succeeds in springing some surprises on us which, in retrospect, seem not only extremely well motivated but delightfully inevitable. It is impossible to lose the thread of dramatic discourse for the action is always unambiguous, the dialogue deliciously crisp, and the comic interest constant. Even if Soyinka had written nothing else, this theatrical gem would have won him a reputation as one of Africa's most extravagantly talented playwrights.

A Dance of the Forests is a different story, so different in fact that it is difficult to determine precisely what Soyinka is driving at most of the time. The meaning of the action is often hidden behind cleverly veiled allusions and slippery symbols which seem to change shape and significance as the transmogrifytes who inhabit the play move about freely in space and time. One has to struggle to remember that X in one context is equal or analogous to Y in another and that either or both may be reincarnations of Z in yet another world. Disguise, duplicity, metamorphosis and revelation are recurring motifs in the plotless plot, and as one moves deeper and deeper into the tangled jungle of events one becomes totally lost in their complications and endless ramifications. One vaguely comprehends that Soyinka is expressing impatience with what he once termed, "the recurrent cycle of human stupidity,"[6] that he seems to believe that history—perhaps especially on historic occasions—has a tendency to repeat its worst blunders, and that he passionately wants human beings to be less vile than they are and always have been. But this message has to be artificially abstracted from the incoherence of the drama by those who happen to know the occasion for which it was written. The kernel idea behind the play—if indeed there is one—[7] is incapable of disseminating itself. This is a pity for there are several scenes of intense dramatic power which could have been harnessed to serve a larger purpose than that of merely keeping an audience visually entertained. Soyinka, by attempting to be sly and subtle at every turn, frittered away theatrical opportunities that might have made this a telling play. As it stands now, it tells us far too little.

It is possible, of course, to explain away this kind of failure by describing *A Dance of the Forests* as a youthful experiment, an aberration of an unseasoned playwright's imperfectly controlled imagination. This was a time, remember, when Soyinka was apparently worried about sending his audience home bored. Because he was striving to be ultraclever so as to sustain the interest of the super-sophisticated, he found it expedient to sacrifice simple communication and speak in prolonged riddles. The plan backfired disastrously. The intellectuals soon discovered they could understand the play no better than the masses, who admitted they understood it not at all, and the whole arty structure collapsed under the oppressive weight of its own topheaviness. One should perhaps forgive and forget such catastrophes. Every young playwright, after all, is entitled to fall flat on his face at least once in his career. The surprising thing is that a dramatist as talented and resourceful as Soyinka had proven himself to be in *The Lion and the Jewel* should make such a horrible mistake.

Soyinka's three short plays, published in the same year as his first two long ones, provide ample evidence that *A Dance of the Forests* was not characteristic of his early writing. *The Trials of Brother Jero,* a rollicking farce about a charlatan masquerading as a beach prophet, had all the comic clarity and raw vigor of *The Lion and the Jewel. The Swamp Dwellers* was a moodier piece, but the gradual unfolding of the drama left no doubt about where Soyinka's moral sympathies lay. *The Strong Breed,* a story about scapegoats and self-sacrifice, occasionally veered into melodrama and ambiguity but Soyinka managed to hold fairly firmly to a clean narrative line which anyone could follow. There were brief flirtations with symbolism, sporadic attempts at indirect commununication in these plays but nothing so inscrutably gnomic as to prepare us for the dense wilderness of words into which we were thrust in *A Dance of the Forests.*

Soyinka's next major play, *The Road* (1965), thus came as something of a surprise and disappointment to many of his followers, for here was the intellectual trickster playing hide-and-seek with his audience again, pursuing what seemed to be the least promising of all the theatrical paths he had travelled before. The old obfuscator had returned and was once more challenging the world to discover the meaning of his art, to unravel its mysteries and knit all its loose, dangling threads into a harmonious pattern. The burden of interpretation fell entirely on the receiver, not the transmitter, of the dramatically coded message, and to do his job properly, a receiver had to stay on his toes at all times, analyze every utterance and gesture, track each image to its logical hideout in the forest of symbols, and ensure that no stray nuance escaped his careful scrutiny, for only by remaining vigilant and alert to every detail could he hope to crack the cipher and locate the tiny key that would unlock the treasure chest of well-preserved secrets. The job was not impossible, for many clues had been strewn throughout the text, but it took more than an ordinary literary detective to solve so cerebral a case. The average theatergoer, tired perhaps from standing too long on his toes or from listening to a language he did not perfectly understand, either fell asleep or trudged home yawning. Direct communication never took place.

This is not to say the play had no immediacy. Like almost everything Soyinka has written, there were bright sparks of life throughout. Indeed, it is conceivable that *The Road* could be enjoyed as a series of well-paced theatrical happenings, even though these actions would not make much sense to John Doe. Soyinka is the kind of polished dramatist who can apply a very slick surface to the roughest or least substantial of narrative foundations. He doesn't need a straight story line to keep us fascinated. The interactions between his characters are so cunningly conceived that scenes move along on their own robust momentum, spin on their own axes of significance. They need not be closely integrated with other events because each episode has an integrity which enables it to stand virtually alone. This is the sort of histrionic razzle-dazzle that makes even Soyinka's failures intriguing to critics, scholars and other connoisseurs of chaos. The body somehow just keeps on moving even though the head is dead.

Not dead exactly, but buried in the sands of its own selfconcealment. *The Road* refuses to yield itself to easy interpretation. It is a defiantly difficult play which makes no compromises with instant intelligibility. The focal character, an absurdly enigmatic professor, behaves as if he has just stepped out of a play by Ionesco or Beckett. He is on a symbolic quest in search of "the Word" which he describes on various occasions as "companion not to life, but Death" (11), "a golden nugget on the tongue" (44), "that elusive kernel...the Key, the moment of my rehabilitation" (63), "a terrible fire" (68). From these conflicting metaphorical definitions it is probably safe to conclude that the Word is some form of cabalistic wisdom which is precious, powerful and associated with death and redemption. The Professor hopes to find the Word by meticulously studying several bundles of newspapers he carries around with him and collecting misplaced roadsigns which have led to fatal highway accidents. He presides over a motor park inhabited by unemployed drivers, touts and thugs for whom he occasionally does small favors such as forging driver's licences and locating automobile wrecks they can strip and plunder. He has as his personal servant a mute young spirit named Murano who has been run over and killed by a lorry not long before the play opens. It turns out that two of the lay-abouts in the motor park are responsible for Murano's death. On this frail but original fictive line Soyinka hangs his drama, letting it balloon and flutter in a gale of gusty words. Here is a typical exchange from this atypical verbal universe:

KOTONU:	If I may ask, Professor, where did you find Murano?
PROF.:	Neglected in the back of a hearse. And dying. Moaned like a dog whose legs have been broken by a motor car. I took him—somewhere—looked after him till he was well again.
KOTONU:	And you set him to tap palm wine for you?
PROF.:	[*rises, goes over to Kotonu.*]: I think you are an astute man, or simply desperate. You grope towards Murano, the one person in this world in whom the Word reposes.
SAMSON:	Much use that is to him. He cannot use his tongue.
PROF.:	Deep. Silent but deep. Oh my friend, beware the pity of those that have no tongue for they have been proclaimed sole guardians of the Word. They have slept beyond the portals of secrets. They have pierced the guard of eternity and unearthed the Word, a golden nugget on the tongue. And so their tongue hangs heavy and they are forever silenced. Do you mean you do not see that Murano has one leg longer than the other?
SAMSON:	Murano? But his legs are the same.
PROF.:	Blind!
KOTONU:	Oh I admit he limps. Anyway he seems okay to me.

PROF.: When a man has one leg in each world, his legs are never the same. The big toe of Murano's foot—the left one of course—rests on the slumbering chrysalis of the Word. When that crust cracks my friends—you and I, that is the moment we await. That is the moment of our rehabilitation. When that crust cracks...[*Growing rapidly emotional, he stops suddenly, sniffs once or twice, wipes his misted glasses, returns briskly to his table.*]

SAMSON: [*goes over to Kotonu.*]: I have often thought of following that Murano you know. He sets out about five o'clock in the morning, goes in that direction. And he doesn't come back until five in the afternoon. That's a long time to tap a little wine. Have you ever considered where he goes?

KOTONU: Why should I?

SAMSON: One of these days I will follow him some of the way...

PROF.: [*sharply.*]: You are tired of life perhaps?

SAMSON: I didn't say anything.

PROF.: Those who are not equipped for strange sights—fools like you—go mad or blind when their curiosity is pursued. First find the Word. It is not enough to follow Murano at dawn and spy on him like a vulgar housewife. Find the Word.

SAMSON: [*disinterested.*]: Where does one find it Professor?

PROF.: Where? Where ascent is broken and a winged secret plummets back to earth. Ask Murano.

SAMSON: But he cannot talk.

PROF.: [*cunningly.*]: You see. They know what they are doing (44-45).[8]

It is possible to enjoy such dialogue at a superficial level as a nicely articulated interchange between insanity and common sense. The Professor and his motor park underlings are obviously on different wave lengths, the professor flying high in the rarified atmosphere of colorful metaphysics while Samson and Kotonu sit grounded in black and white realities. Samson and Kotonu cannot fathom what the Professor says, and the Professor is in the habit of overinterpreting what they say, reading deeper significance than they intended into their utterances. The audience, aware of the vast intellectual gulf that separates the speakers and keeps their conversation from connecting, may be amused by the sheer futility of their interaction, possibly recognizing in it a reflection of the total breakdown of communication that can occur in any society between the uneducated and the over-educated. So at the most elementary theatrical level, the level of simple entertainment, this scene can be appreciated, perhaps even thoroughly enjoyed, by someone who does not understand a word the Professor says. The action has enough integrity to seem weirdly real. This is the magic of Soyinka's stage touch.

But of course the dialogue is not barren of significance. The Professor's statements are pregnant with meaning and carry the seed of his most seminal ideas about life and death. Murano, we learn, is in some sort of purgatory or halfway house for newly-deceased souls. Being neither completely dead nor minimally alive, he has already acquired the ontological knowledge the Professor desires but he cannot pass it on to anyone in the land of the living. An ordinary mortal like Samson who wants to follow Murano to learn his secret would risk death or insanity if he did so. The greatest challenge confronting thinking man is to discover the meaning of life by comprehending the mystery of death. This is the challenge the Professor takes up, the Word he seeks. He is another Dr. Faustus attempting to overreach the natural boundaries of human intelligence.

An interpretation of this sort is possible if we have the text before us and can read carefully between the lines. But it is doubtful that anyone watching the play would be alert enough to grasp the full significance of the Professor's statements and be able simultaneously to piece together the history of Murano's gradual metamorphosis in death from vaguely corporeal to entirely ethereal spirit. The metaphysical context in which the drama is set is too unfamiliar for a non-Yoruba audience to assimilate rapidly, and the conventions and techniques which

Soyinka shares with European "theater of the absurd" might make portions of the play very difficult for a Yoruba audience to comprehend. Perhaps I am underestimating the typical Yoruba playgoer, but I daresay he, like the rest of us, must find it far easier to cope with the neat geometry of *The Lion and the Jewel* than with the complex symbolic structure of *The Road*. He too must often feel in sympathy with Samson who had the honesty to complain "You are a very confusing person Professor. I can't follow you at all" (63).

Which brings us back to the question of Soyinka's audience. For whom did he build *The Road*? Was it just for Westernized Yoruba eggheads, was it for a cosmopolitan international elite, or could it have been simply for himself?[9] Why did he ascend the ivory tower and lock himself up in one of its least accessible compartments?

A partial answer to some of these questions can be sought in his next full-length play which was much more down-to-earth. *Kongi's Harvest* (1967) was a biting political satire aimed at exposing the egomaniacal fatuity of modern African leaders. When the play opens, Kongi has already assumed dictatorial control of Isma, a new nation-state, and he is trying to bring recalcitrant traditional rulers under his thumb. He meets with stubborn opposition from Oba Danlola, a wily old chief who refuses to make the required public display of loyalty and subservience to the new regime. Kongi's delusions of grandeur and dreams of building monuments to celebrate his own magnificence are eventually shattered when he is toppled from power by Oba Danlola's supporters. Tyranny gets its just desserts in this pointed political parable. What marks this play as different from *The Road* and *A Dance of the Forests* is not just the explicitly political theme but the immediate intelligibility of the dramatic action. We always know what's going on in Isma because Soyinka doesn't hide anything from us. He seems to realize that clarity is a prerequisite for forceful protest. One is tempted to conclude that when Soyinka has a political grumble to voice he knows exactly which register to use to deliver it most effectively. He is not a prisoner of his own private imagery; he can still go public whenever the occasion warrants it. Perhaps it would be fair to say that when he feels philosophical, he turns inward, when political, outward.

But a more recent play, *Madmen and Specialists* (1971), tends to belie this. Here Soyinka seems to be struggling to make a political point about the dehumanizing effects of war but he blunts the force of his idea by wrapping it in the idiom of obscurity. One still recognizes in certain scenes and lines his characteristic contempt for that compulsively destructive human tendency he once called "cannibalism,"[10] an all-consuming dog-eat-dog mentality evidenced in the play in Dr. Bero's predatory boast that during the war he literally acquired a taste for human flesh. One also sees flashes of Soyinka's hatred for any form of tyranny and for the trembling sycophancy that encourages it. But these are sidewise glimpses into a multi-faceted cryptograph, and they do not begin to tell the whole story. The verbal texture of the play is perhaps its most bewildering aspect, for the strategy of repartee often seems to be predicated on little more than a proliferation of puns. Here is a simple sample:

CRIPPLE: (*slowly releasing a puff of smoke*). Oh, that feels good. Haven't had such a good puff since that corpulent First Lady visited us and passed round imported cigarettes.

GOYI: The Old Man was mad for days. Suckers, he called us. Quite right too. Good smoke is a good suck. I wasn't going to throw away that superior brand just to please a crackpot.

AAFAA: Hey, remember the song the Old Man wrote to celebrate the occasion? Visit of the First Lady to the Home for the de-balled.

BLINDMAN: ...for the Disabled.

AAFAA: Bloody pendant.

BLINDMAN: Pe-dant.

AAFAA: (*gives up*). Oh Christ! (55-56).[11]

The punning becomes even more furious toward the end of the play where there are long, babbling monologues:

> OLD MAN: ...we are together in As. (*He rises slowly.*) As Is, and the System is its mainstay though it wear a hundred masks and a thousand outward forms. And because you are within the System, the cyst in the System that irritates, the foul gurgle of the cistern, the expiring function of a faulty cistern and are part of the material for re-formulating the mind of a man into the necessity of the moment's political As, the moment's scientific As, metaphysic As, sociologic As, economic, recreative ethical As, you-cannot-es-cape! (71-72).

This is only a warm up. The Old Man's concluding curse is a parade of unparalleled paronomasia:

> ...you cyst, you cyst, you splint in the arrow of arrogance, the dog in dogma, tick of a heretic, the tick in politics, the mock of democracy, the mar of marxism, a tic of the fanatic, the boo in buddhism, the ham in Mohammed, the dash in the criss-cross of Christ, a dot on the i of ego, an ass in the mass, the ash in ashram, a boot in kibbutz, the pee of priesthood, the peepee of perfect priesthood, oh how dare you raise your hindquarters you dog of dogma and cast the scent of your existence on the lamp-post of Destiny you HOLE IN THE ZERO of NOTHING! (76).

These puns are fun and likely to tickle any audience, but on closer inspection they may be viewed with sober apprehension as representing a very dangerous tendency in Soyinka's art—a tendency toward meaningless frivolity which robs his work of any serious implication. Soyinka seems content to settle for the short-term gain of a giggle or bellylaugh rather than work towards any long-range effect that will leave a more profound impression on his audience. In *Madmen and Specialists* he is playing mostly to the pit, not caring whether the fantasies spun on stage will make any significant difference in the lives of those who witness them. This is clowning for clowning's sake, and whatever political idea or attitude may be imbedded in the play is lost in the freakish circus atmosphere Soyinka creates. The message is smothered by the medium.

Ali Mazrui once argued that Soyinka's countryman, the late Christopher Okigbo, was too obscure a poet for Africa.

> To put it bluntly, Africa cannot afford too many Okigbos. She cannot afford many versifiers the bulk of whose poems are untranslatable, and whose genius lies in imagery and music rather than conversational meaning...One can only hope he does not produce too many imitators after him. His was the kind of genius which must remain fundamentally a luxury. A limited amount of it is deeply satisfying and is a great adornment to culture. A massive outpouring of this particular kind of genius could, however, destroy a literary civilization.[12]

The same argument could be made about Soyinka as a playwright. Indeed, his obscurity is even more lamentable than Okigbo's because he is working in the most public of the literary arts. A poet or novelist communicates privately with his audience by scratching words on paper. Contrary to what Mazrui thinks, it may not really matter too much if such an artist lapses into esoteric mumbo-jumbo or takes gross liberties with form and technique so that few can understand him because by the very act of choosing a bookish medium he has already quite severely limited his potential audience to a very small fraction of the total African population: the educated elite who read for pleasure.[13] This tiny minority will be sophisticated enough to appreciate radical experiments in literary "modernity" or, if they find an author too precious or impenetrable, will certainly have the good sense to stop reading him. The poet or novelist without an urgent message to communicate can therefore afford to be eccentric because hardly anyone will notice what he is doing anyway. His art is an unnecessary pastime appreciated only by a handful of kindred souls in the upper strata of his society.

But the dramatist can speak to a much wider audience because he writes for the stage rather than for the page. He is the only writer who can be understood by the illiterate masses, the only one who can take full advantage of performing arts in which Africans unquestionably excel—song, dance, instrumental music, mime, ritual. This gives him powerful social and artistic leverage if he uses his resources well. But if he wastes his opportunities by indulging in pretentious, indecipherable charades, he will betray his people and destroy the public value of his art. The African dramatist who refuses to write in a genuinely African idiom for the largest possible African audience is evading his moral and social responsibilities. He will never become a seer, never succeed in leading his society to greater sanity, if he persists in whispering his words to the wind.

Soyinka once said that "the poet insists on mysteries only at the peril of truth."[14] For the dramatist the stakes are even higher, for he risks losing the life as well as truth of his art if he clothes it in opaque obscurity. Soyinka would do well to heed his own warning and stop squandering his immense wealth of talent on fashionable theatrical trivialities. He may be Africa's greatest playwright but one suspects he could be even greater if he were more nakedly African.

NOTES

1. Soyinka has frequently said he does not consider himself a committed writer. See, for example, the interviews published in *Spear* (May 1966), p. 17, and *African Writers Talking*, ed. Dennis Duerden and Cosmo Pieterse (New York: Africana, 1972), p. 173. However, he often behaves and writes like a committed writer.

2. "The Writer in a Modern African State," *The Writer in Modern Africa*, ed. Per Wästberg (Uppsala: Scandinavian Institute of African Studies, 1968), pp. 15-16. The same essay was published in *Transition*, 31 (1967), 11-13.

3. Ibid., p. 21.

4. Ibid., p. 58.

5. Duerden and Pieterse, pp. 172-73.

6. Wästberg, p. 20.

7. Soyinka has said that the main thing at the back of his mind when writing *A Dance of the Forests* was his "personal conviction or observation that human beings are simply cannibals all over the world so that their main preoccupation seems to be eating up one another." See Duerden and Pieterse, p. 173.

8. *The Road* (London: Oxford University Press, 1965). All quotations are from this edition.

9. In an interview in *Spear* (May 1966), p. 18, Soyinka spoke of *The Road* as "one of the three personal plays I have written...It is based on what I might call a personal intimacy with a certain aspect of the road...which developed out of my travels on the road. It was almost a kind of exorcism writing that play."

10. See footnote 7.

11. *Madmen and Specialists* (Ibadan: Oxford University Press, 1971). All quotations are from this edition.

12. Ali A. Mazrui, "Meaning versus Imagery in African Poetry," *Présence Africaine*, 66 (1968), 57. This argument was first articulated by Mazrui in "Abstract Verse and African Tradition," *Zuka*, 1 (1967), 47-49.

13. For a discussion of the reading habits of African intellectuals, see Chinua Achebe, "What do African Intellectuals Read?" *Times Literary Supplement*, 12 May 1972, p. 547.

14. Wole Soyinka, "And After the Narcissist?" *African Forum*, 1, 4 (1966), 53.

Ngugi wa Thiong'o's Early Journalism

Ngugi wa Thiong'o (formerly James Ngugi) entered Makerere University College in 1959 and began his literary career toward the end of 1960 by contributing a short story entitled "The Fig Tree" to *Penpoint*, the university English Department's literary magazine.[1] His next story "The Wind" was published three months later in both *Penpoint* and the *Kenya Weekly News*, a European settlers' magazine based in Nairobi.[2] From this modest beginning, Ngugi went on in 1961 to compose three more stories[3] as well as the first draft of a novel he called "The Black Messiah," which he entered in a novel-writing competition sponsored by the East African Literature Bureau. Ngugi's manuscript garnered the top prize in the English-language section of the competition and subsequently was revised and published in 1965 as *The River Between*.[4]

But even before winning this competition and getting published in Heinemann's newly established African Writers Series, Ngugi had become fairly well-known locally as a promising author. By the middle of 1961 his stories had already attracted a modicum of printed critical attention. The Assistant Editor of the *Kenya Weekly News* had been quoted as saying, "Mr. Ngugi writes well because his stories are truly characteristic of Africans and their surroundings."[5] And one of Ngugi's peers at Makerere had publicly expressed the opinion that

> This young writer makes his stories deal with the day-to-day life in the villages—problems caused by drought, the village medicine-man versus an African priest, the tension between the old and the

> new ways of life and so on. His success indicates that the secret lies in dealing with reality—with or without an African background.[6]

All this acclaim must have been very encouraging to a twenty-three-year-old undergraduate who had wanted to write when he was in secondary school but had "never actually got down to it until [he] got to University."[7] The following year he was even more productive, writing his second novel *Weep Not, Child*,[8] short stories for the lively, new, Kampala-based magazine *Transition* and the Cape Town "radical review" *The New African*,[9] and at least three plays that were staged at Makerere.[10] A *Kenya Weekly News* preview of the most ambitious of these plays, "The Black Hermit," stated that

> Mr. J. T. Ngugi, the author, is a young Makerere undergraduate with a proud, though short, record in the world of writing. As a playwright he is well known to Makerere and Kampala audiences, especially through his "The Rebels," and "This Wound in My Heart," which won the English competition in the College this year. Incidentally I hear "This Wound in My Heart," which was to appear in the Uganda Drama Festival, has been rejected by the censors. "It is the usual practice for the censors to inform the author why his play has been rejected but I have so far not been told anything," Mr. Ngugi told me.[11]

Apparently, even at this early stage in his literary career, Ngugi was having trouble with government authorities—a portent of the difficulties he was to face in 1977 when he was arrested and detained for producing a play he had co-authored with Ngugi wa Mirii in Kikuyu, *Ngaahika Ndeenda* (I will marry when I want).

This brief account of the first few years of Ngugi's literary career, concentrating as it does on the two genres—fiction and drama—in which he was to make a major impact on the East African literary scene, would not be complete without some consideration of a third form of writing that he engaged in extensively as an undergraduate: journalism. Between May 1961 and August 1964 Ngugi wrote nearly eighty pieces for the Nairobi press, contributing first to the *Sunday Post*, then preparing a fairly regular weekly or fortnightly column for the *Sunday Nation*, and finally working fulltime as a "Junior Reporter" and editorial commentator for the *Daily Nation* in the months between his graduation from Makerere and his departure for postgraduate studies at Leeds University in England.[12] Ngugi's *Sunday Nation* column, entitled "As I See It," was meant to represent an African point of view, just as a parallel column written under the same title by N.S. Toofan was intended to provide a voice for Kenya's Asians. As time went on, Ngugi's views were given more prominence by being moved from the back pages to page 5 or 6 of the paper. When he joined the regular *Nation* staff, he also wrote a column of "Commentary" for the daily paper and a column of "Kenya Commentary" for the Sunday edition. It is interesting to look back at these pieces today to see what they reveal of Ngugi's attitudes and opinions in the early 1960s.

One must remember that these were very heady years in East Africa. The period between 1961 and 1963 saw political independence come to Tanganyika, Uganda, Zanzibar and Kenya, and only a few weeks after Ngugi left for England in 1964, Tanganyika and Zanzibar merged to form Tanzania. These individual countries, though independent, remained members of a closely-knit East African community of nations, for a time sharing common transportation and communications systems and a common currency. Unity was more than a slogan to the leading nationalist politicians of that era who had led their areas of the world to self-rule. The political events in all the East African countries were reported in detail in the Nairobi newspapers of the day.

Ngugi started contributing articles to the *Sunday Post* shortly after two of his early stories had appeared in the *Kenya Weekly News*. Four of the five journalistic pieces he wrote in mid-1961 dealt with literary or cultural topics, but he also ventured to touch on sensitive social and political problems. He made his debut with an essay entitled "'The African Personality' is a Delusion:

Do Tigers have 'Tigritude'?"[13] in which he attacked Kwame Nkrumah's concept of a racially distinctive "African Personality" as a "political adulteration of Negritude" that had no foundation in fact. While conceding that Africans "had identical grievances and struggles against Colonialism and Imperialism," Ngugi did not feel that these common political experiences gave Africans a personality or oneness. He warned that

> with the rise of African nationalism, we are in danger of replacing one racial myth with an identical one, only this time, it would be of our own making. [Here] is an assumption or a belief that in some way the African is unique, this time not in an "inferior" way, but in a "superior" way. I personally do not believe in anything uniquely superior, or inferior, in any one race, or group of people, whatever the color of their skin, or country of their origin...I would say that any assertion that there is an absolute personality which uniquely and inherently belongs to a people, just because they happen to be black and colonized, is just racialism well disguised...I believe in the personality of men, and not of race.

Ngugi then concluded the essay by citing an amusing remark he had heard at the university:

> Mr. Acheke [sic], the young Nigerian novelist, speaking to a group of Makerere students, quoted somebody as saying that a tiger does not sing about its "tigritude." It was a comment on Negritude.

Thus, in his earliest published piece of nonfictional prose, Ngugi explored a controversial cultural issue by spurning the ideas of two African Heads of State, Kwame Nkrumah and Léopold Sédar Senghor, and aligning himself with the opinions of Chinua Achebe and Wole Soyinka, authors as yet not widely known in East Africa. In political stance and literary education he was already ahead of his time.

Some of Ngugi's early literary interests were revealed in his next essay for the *Sunday Post*, "The New Voices: Some Emerging African Writers,"[14] in which he commented on works by Peter

Abrahams, Noni Jabavu, Amos Tutuola, Cyprian Ekwensi, Chinua Achebe and William Conton. He singled out two problems facing aspiring African writers—language and audience, both of which were awkwardly foreign unless one wrote for the "small public" able to read an African vernacular. But in an autobiographical introduction to his essay Ngugi dramatized an even more crippling problem confronting highly educated Africans who had literary ambitions:

> The lantern light flickered slightly, setting up ghostly shadows which flitted across the mud-walls of the round hut. The table was long and narrow. My friend sat opposite me.
>
> "...So you are going to College?"
>
> "Yes."
>
> "What are you going to take?"
>
> "English."
>
> He looked hard at me. He frowned a little and seemed puzzled. A pause. Then in an accusing tone of deep incredulity and surprise, he exclaimed:
>
> "What on earth for?"
>
> "Well, I would like to use English and write beautiful stories about people, birds etc, etc."
>
> He knew I meant it. He stood up, glaring hard at me, almost foaming with fury.
>
> "You fool." At last he managed to say, "Why don't you take medicine or law—something that could be of use to our people?" And that rather nicely sums it up. It partly explains why over the past years so little in the way of creative writing has been done by Africans.

In the face of such a reaction, especially at a time of profound political transformation when public attention was being focused on the need for qualified manpower to assist in the rapid development of modern nation-states in Africa, it must have taken some courage and determination to persist in pursuing a literary vocation, as Ngugi did.

That he did not lack true grit was evident in his next journalistic contribution, a piece on the tendency of educated Africans who are "disillusioned with the western way of life" to "look back and see an Ideal African culture—now lost. They want to revive it—revive the culture of their ancestors."[15] This understandable tendency to glorify the past as a Golden Age was particularly noticeable among Negritude poets, but it could also be glimpsed in a book written by Kenya's most famous author. In a passage underscored for emphasis Ngugi wrote:

> *The past tends to be seen through a distorted mirror. Read through "Facing Mount Kenya" and one sees the same tendency with Kenyatta.*

Such words, printed in August 1961, the very month that Jomo Kenyatta was finally released from all political restraints following nine years of detention in a colonial prison, must have been quite shocking. Even though the essay did not focus primarily on Kenyatta, the European editors of the *Sunday Post* decided to give it a bold, eye-catching title: "African Culture: The Mistake that Kenyatta Made." The "mistake" was spelled out in a subtitle: "There is no going back to the past."

This was too much for Ngugi. The following week the *Sunday Post* carried a letter from him expressing his desire "to correct one or two wrong impressions which may have been given to some readers by the headline on my article on African Culture."[16] He explained that he had not intended to suggest that "Kenyatta had at one time advocated a return to the past"; rather, he had stated that *Facing Mount Kenya*, a scholarly work "which treats the Kikuyu way of life with the greatest amount of sympathy and understanding," shared a widespread human tendency to "idealize the past." The book was a nostalgic view of Kikuyu culture, not an atavistic call for a regression to tribal traditions. Ngugi tried to make it clear that he admired Kenyatta "as an African writer who will for a long time remain in the forefront of those intellectuals who have tried to interpret their way of life to the world." He was applauding Kenyatta the anthropologist, not condemning Kenyatta the politician.

Ngugi wrote one more piece for the *Sunday Post*, an essay on "Social Problems Of the New Villages,"[17] before resuming his studies at Makerere in September 1961. It dealt with the consequences of colonial land consolidation in Kikuyuland, particularly the social and moral problems arising from landlessness and widespread unemployment. He noted that the hungry, deprived inhabitants of these overcrowded villages were waiting patiently for Uhuru because they expected to see a "magic transformation overnight" once Africans were governing Kenya. Ngugi thus anticipated the bitter disillusionment that ordinary Kenyans were to feel after independence when their exaggerated expectations were not fulfilled. The gloom and pessimism he later expressed in such novels as *A Grain of Wheat* and *Petals of Blood* may have been rooted in the unhappy accuracy of his prognosis on the future ills of his society.

After publishing this piece of social commentary, Ngugi did not write articles for the Kenya press for the next nine months. This would have been the time when he was finishing off the first draft of *The River Between* as well as beginning *Weep Not, Child* and staging his first plays. However, in March of 1962 a correspondent for the *Kenya Weekly News* reported that

> The other day, when a Kenya English newspaper appealed to Makerere for students who might be interested in working on it, I hear that there were more applicants than all Kenya newspapers could afford to employ.[18]

It appears that this newspaper was the *Sunday Nation* and the successful applicant J.T. Ngugi, for his articles began to appear in it regularly two months later.

The first piece he wrote was on education,[19] a theme that dominates both of his early novels. One can hear echoes of *Weep Not, Child* in the opening paragraphs:

> I remember the first boy to go to a secondary school from our village. It happened in 1952 and created quite a sensation. His name and fame spread from ridge to ridge like a bush fire.
>
> An elder speaking to those of us who were left, declared: "The future belongs to the educated man." I have heard this now on many occasions.
>
> But I still remember the elder and his voice full of passion, for it was then I knew that the boy who cleared the educational hurdle of the KAPE was to be admired and envied.
>
> Education made this boy a hero, rocketed him from the insignificant society of "one of us" to a society of "them"—the educated "them."
>
> The position of the educated African has been variedly discussed and it is a proud mother who has a son in this position.

Education was a topic Ngugi returned to often in his column. He strongly advocated adult education, urged that schools be racially integrated and teachers better paid, agitated for major changes in the school syllabus to make the curriculum more relevant to Africa, suggested that French be studied at East African universities, and complained about the divisiveness that mission education introduced into African communities. Occasionally further echoes of the educational ideas he elaborated in his fiction reverberated in the *Sunday Nation*. In an article on Ugandan private schools,[20] for instance, he commented on the popular attitude toward education when he was growing up in Kenya:

> Education was then, as it is now, the African's God Number Two. Uhuru and Land were Number One. Many politicians said so, anyway.

This makes one think of Waiyaki's plight in *The River Between*, just as an earlier article pleading for the abolition of the "brutal" custom of clitoridectomy reminds one of Muthoni and Nyambura in the same novel.[21]

However, as might be expected during a period of intense nationalism, Ngugi's journalism tended to be preoccupied with politics, his orientation at this time being more liberal than radical. He came out against racialism, tribalism, regionalism and censorship, and championed such causes as old age pensions, enlightened peasant agriculture, strong labor unions, national policy planning, and women's rights. Considering his later post-Leeds shift to a more extreme leftist position on social and political matters, it is rather surprising to find in some of his early writing a condemnation of the Land Freedom Army,[22] an endorsement of western Christianity as "the best challenge to Communism or any form of totalitarianism,"[23] and a stern warning against sending Kenyan students "to any obscure half-civilized country that calls itself Communistic and Socialistic."[24] Of course, any writer is likely to change a number of his opinions over time, but some he may never vary. In Ngugi's case, the constants seem to be particular social attitudes: sympathy for the common man, faith in formal education, yearning for political unity and interracial harmony, and delight in evidence of human progress.

In examining Ngugi's early ideas, it is interesting to note the range and variety of the sources he quotes. Many of them are decidedly literary and reflect the reading he was required to do at Makerere—Lawrence, Conrad, Arnold, Dickens, Shelley, Shakespeare. One even finds him defending the study of Shakespeare in African schools by asserting that

> Shakespeare...is very much alive today. The political and moral issues he raises, are most relevant to East Africa. The society in which he wrote was, in so many ways, similar to ours...Shakespeare was not afraid to probe into that society; to express in poetic and dramatic terms the tensions and conflicts within the community...These questions that preoccupied Shakespeare 400 years ago will be the sort of questions to which our emerging writers will have to address themselves. And they need to capture the compelling urgency of Shakespeare if they are to give a sense of

> moral direction to our young countries in their search for order and stability.[25]

Although Ngugi today would still insist that African writers must give moral direction to their countries, it is doubtful that he would cite Shakespeare as a model to be emulated. He would probably select an example closer to home.

It is clear that Ngugi was also reading whatever African literature was available to him in the early 1960s. In addition to the African writers already mentioned, there are references in his essays to Damas, Mphahlele, Nyerere, J. P. Clark, and the African-American author James Baldwin. In a piece on the responsibility of the press, Ngugi criticized Nicholas Montsarrat's *The Tribe that Lost its Head* as "a crude novel with a lot of intellectual dishonesty or escapism. It depicts African nationalism as all savagery."[26] Yet in an essay on censorship he was willing to defend Robert Ruark's equally racist novel *Uhuru* from Government banning, even though he admitted it contained "nothing of value."[27] It is inconceivable that these authors would have been studied in courses at Makerere so Ngugi must have been doing a lot of reading on his own.

There is no evidence to indicate that he had discovered Frantz Fanon, George Lamming, Marcus Garvey or many other Caribbean writers yet, so one must assume that he started reading them a few years later at the University of Leeds. Karl Marx is also conspicuously absent from his Makerere writings.

What may have done more than anything else to stimulate Ngugi to continue his efforts at creative writing was the Conference of African Writers of English Expression held at Makerere in June of 1962. Participating were Chinua Achebe, J.P. Clark, Gabriel Okara, Christopher Okigbo and Wole Soyinka of Nigeria; Kofi Awoonor and Cameron Duodu of Ghana; Ezekiel Mphahlele, Bloke Modisane, Arthur Maimane and Lewis Nkosi of South Africa; Langston Hughes and Saunders Redding of the United States; and a score of other writers, critics and scholars from Dahomey, Cameroon, England, the West Indies, and East

Africa. Ngugi registered his excitement in a report on the conference published in both the *Sunday Nation* and *Transition*:[28]

> It is always something for a creative writer to feel that he is not working in isolation and that there are many others on the same venture.
>
> All of [the writers at the conference] struck me as being expectant and dedicated to writing.
>
> Indeed they are the black heralds of a new awareness in the emergent Africa.

He then made a remark bordering on prophecy:

> I think...that one of the important things about the conference was the fact that it was held in East Africa.
>
> What may be born here and grow as a result is yet too early to predict. I have no doubt that writers from East Africa will rise. The few that I met at Kampala were very enthusiastic and eager to push ahead.

It was Ngugi himself who pushed ahead most vigorously in the next few years, giving East Africa its first significant literary works in English.

Another of Ngugi's remarks about the conference does not appear in retrospect to have been quite so prophetic, however. Noting that "the whole conference was almost quiet on such things as colonialism, imperialism and other -isms," he applauded the fact that the African writer could now confidently turn his attention to other things and try to create out of the material at hand "something living and lasting." He quoted with approval a comment one of the delegates had made about a poem by J.P. Clark:

> Here is no gesture of political or historical protest, no advice, no statement even of the poet's color or its significance; but a faithful and beautifully controlled account of individual experience.

Ngugi found this attitude quite exhilarating, seeing in it "a landmark in the cultural reawakening of our continent." He concluded by stating that "with the death of colonialism, a new society is being born. And with it a new literature." Today he probably would want to redefine what had been born and what had died.

The notion that politics can interfere with art was developed further by Ngugi six months later in an article focusing primarily on the predicament of the South African writer.[29] A black or colored writer from this part of the continent

> cannot ignore the political humiliation of many of his color—who are denied their place in the country of their birth.
>
> Such a state where man is never at peace and lives in fear of being arrested becomes intolerable.
>
> The writer is forced to resort to protest writing—to stories of violence, restlessness and hunger for freedom.
>
> But this situation places the creative writer in a sharp difficulty. The race situation is one which is easy to exploit.
>
> Type characters are there. Even before the writer has set his pen on the paper he has a public which is ready to sympathize with the situation. The battle is half done. It is easy to sit down and relax. No need to sweat. No need to examine and explore every corner of human experience.
>
> The South African writer is, of course, aware of the predicament. He knows that if he succumbs to the temptation of using type situations and characters, his writing will remain mediocre—at best a social documentation, of interest only to students of politics and sociology.

Ngugi went on to discuss Ezekiel Mphahlele's thoughts on this subject as revealed in *The African Image,* and then he tried to show how writers elsewhere in Africa shared a similar plight:

> If the South African writer is in danger of being chained by the desire to protest, the writer in the rest of the continent where there is political freedom is also in danger of other attitudes like Negritude and the desire to assert African personality.

> The talk about the African personality, the desire to assert it and the whole concept of Negritude may have been relevant in the colonial era.
>
> Indeed, this very desire to assert what was good in one's people and their way of life in the face of a world that was not prepared to see the light, placed the African writer of any sort in a dilemma.
>
> Truth demanded that he should be objective and that he should be as critical of his own people and himself, as he was of the ruling powers.
>
> But the fear of being misunderstood by both his fellow Africans and the ruling peoples was great.
>
> He did not want to feel that he had betrayed his people when his criticism of his people was taken as a justification of the white man's way of life and continued domination.
>
> The coming of uhuru has, however, changed the situation...To the African writer who must express the aspirations, failures and successes of a nation on the move, new thinking and fresh outlook are necessary. He has no tradition on which to build.
>
> Protest writing and Negritude are not much of a help. For these are poses and attitudes.
>
> They have left a large area of permanent human experience unexplored...[The African writer] must touch on and capture the intricacies of a human situation with compassion and understanding. Above all he must feel the throb of life in the nation.

Apparently Ngugi himself was less interested in the "poses and attitudes" of protest writing than he was in capturing "the intricacies of a human situation with compassion and understanding" and feeling "the throb of life in the nation." To put it another way, he wanted to concentrate on the individual microcosm rather than the social macrocosm. The "large area of permanent human experience" that he wished to explore in order to discharge his duty to "express the aspirations, failures and successes of a nation on the move" was an area of private actions and emotions, an area that could not be treated honestly in overcharged political rhetoric.

Ngugi expanded on these ideas in other essays, especially several dealing with visual arts and drama. His theme was that the new energy in the country generated by Uhuru should be given a cultural outlet and that less attention should be paid to politics. In fact, one article begins with the statement: "Politics! Politics! Every time we open a newspaper political arguments and quarrels stare us in the face."[30] In another piece entitled "Must we draw Africanness into everything?" Ngugi declares, "I am tired of the talk about 'African socialism.'"[31]

This is not to say that he was opposed to art that was politically engaged or ideologically committed to socialism. In one of these essays[32] he warns against the kind of artistic detachment that becomes

> an escape, something that has nothing to do with people's lives. [The artist] cannot afford to keep himself detached from the problems that are around him.
>
> People's agonies must be his agonies. A nation's joy must be his joy, too...Perhaps it is necessary to repeat that an artist is NOT a hermit. He is concerned with the daily business of living.

Yet the artist's involvement in the daily business of living should be culturally productive. He should do something to uplift his people without misleading them by giving them a false sense of optimism. "Joys and sorrows, happiness and suffering must be captured with sincerity." He should serve his society through his art yet remain independent enough to voice unpopular opinions when necessary. "Above all, the artist must retain his individuality. His art must not give people just what they want."

Ngugi felt that one of the best ways to stimulate "greater practical contributions by Africans to the national culture of our country" was through theatrical activity. He applauded the efforts of amateur groups whose productions he had seen in Nairobi and Kampala, and he tried to encourage the formation of others:

> I suggest that one of the ways in which Africans can help and develop an indigenous drama rooted in the country is by actually writing and producing plays...
>
> Let, therefore, the Africans living in Nairobi come together and form something like an amateur dramatic society whose members should write and act plays.
>
> If they cannot at first get someone to write something for them they can get some works of the two leading Nigerian dramatists—Wole Soyenika [sic] and J. P. Clark and act them for the Nairobi audience.
>
> Last June the Kampala Amateur Dramatic Society produced J. P. Clark's play—*The Song of a Goat*—and there was very good attendance. We in East Africa should have more of this kind of thing.
>
> Is this too much to ask? I don't think so. I believe that there is much talent laying untapped in our country.
>
> Let us now exploit these resources and build a culture that has deep roots in the country.[33]

Ngugi reiterated this plea a year later when he reviewed a Makerere production of *The Lion and the Jewel*, "by Nigeria's leading poet-dramatist, Wole Soyeninka [sic]."[34] He even suggested that the Makerere College Dramatic Society "organize a touring company and show such a play in Nairobi or Dar es Salaam, where African dramatic activities have not yet really started." It was only twelve months after this article was printed that faculty and students launched the Makerere Travelling Theatre, a troupe that staged plays in four languages before enthusiastic audiences not in Nairobi and Dar es Salaam but in many smaller towns and villages scattered throughout Uganda and parts of Western Kenya. A similar troupe, formed at the University of Nairobi several years later, continued making annual tours and enjoying enormous popularity. Ngugi had been right about the great cultural potential and mass appeal of live theater. His own return to playwriting in the late 1970s appears to have been prompted partly by a desire to reach this grass-roots audience.

It may be quite significant that some of Ngugi's more recent pronouncements on writing have been concerned with the need for developing literatures in African languages. Indeed, in 1979 he was involved in a very lively debate in Nairobi on this subject, a debate in which he is reported to have said, "Only going back to the roots of our being in the languages and cultures of the Kenyan people can we rise up to the challenge of helping in the creation of a Kenyan National Culture."[35] This may have been one of his motives for choosing to write his play *Ngaahika Ndeenda* in Kikuyu. But his preoccupation with the issue of seeking an appropriate literary language is nothing new. In an interview recorded at Leeds University in 1967, he spoke of having

> reached a point of crisis. I don't know whether it is worth any longer writing in English...One important social reality in Africa is that 90 per cent of the people cannot read or speak English...The problem is this—I know whom I write about, but whom do I write for?[36]

This attitude is not much different from one he expressed five years earlier in the *Sunday Nation* when writing about the place of Swahili in East Africa.[37] He began by pointing out that

> One of the things African writers complain about is that they are forced to tame the music and strifes in their own souls by having to use a foreign language.
>
> Much of the better-known works by African writers have appeared either in English or French.
>
> And this is not because the African languages are necessarily poor or inferior in forms of expressions to French or English.
>
> The true reasons are not actually far to find. The reading public in Africa is at present very small, especially that for creative literature.
>
> The desire to meet a larger audience outside their homes has meant that these writers must use the languages which will be understood by that larger audience outside.
>
> In other words, the African writers have been catering for a foreign audience. The other reason is that the study of vernacular

> languages especially in secondary schools and colleges has been totally neglected.
>
> This neglect of indigenous languages must remain a black spot in the whole of colonial education in Africa.
>
> In East Africa, for instance, one wonders why Swahili has been so neglected.

After pointing out the virtues of Swahili as a language of education and literary expression, Ngugi issued a challenge "to writers in general and African writers in particular, to produce more and more work in these languages so that there can be enough material for reading and study." However, he qualified his advocacy of indigenous languages by admitting that English also had a legitimate place in African education.

> I do not, of course, suggest that European languages should be neglected or necessarily be given a second place in the school curriculum.
>
> The importance of English, which is daily nearing what may be called a universal language, cannot be overemphasised...
>
> Still, in a place like Kenya we are faced with the fact that for national interests, English, however serviceable, remains inadequate.
>
> A great majority of the people cannot understand it. And so as a medium for daily communication and hence for national unity, English is definitely out...
>
> I do not think for a moment that we can ever be a nation of any importance unless we have a language of our own through which our national aspirations and spiritual growth can be expressed.

In 1962 Ngugi felt that Swahili offered the best opportunity for achieving a "language of our own." In 1979 he felt that Kikuyu was the best option—for him, at least—and that all languages spoken by Kenyan nationals ought to be recognized as National languages.[38] His perspective on language had changed, but only slightly. However, his practices as a writer had changed profoundly. One doubts that Ngugi will return to writing in English in the near future.

Ngugi's early journalism makes interesting reading for anyone desiring to trace the evolution of his literary ideas and social attitudes, for it is a permanent record of his utterances on a variety of important issues at a time when he was on the threshold of his career as an author. Some of his opinions changed considerably as years passed, others did not, and one must try to discern the reasons why in order to comprehend what has happened in East Africa in the last forty years, for he has been one of the best articulators of the dominant intellectual concerns of his generation. Reading Ngugi is thus like reading a detailed history of contemporary East Africa. Anyone seeking to know the full story must begin with the earliest chapters on record.

NOTES

1. *Penpoint*, 9 (December 1960), 3-9. The story begins with a quotation from a poem by D. H. Lawrence.

2. *Penpoint*, 10 (March 1960), 9-13; *Kenya Weekly News*, 17 March 1961, pp. 39, 42.

3. "The Village Priest," *Kenya Weekly News*, 28 April 1961, pp. 44-45, and *Penpoint*, 13 (October 1962), 2-6; "Gone With the Drought!" *Kenya Weekly News*, 2 June 1961, pp. 34, 44, and *Penpoint*, 12 (March 1962), 2-6; "And the Rain Came Down!" *Kenya Weekly News*, 13 October 1961, pp. 36-37. All these early stories except "The Wind," which featured characters who reappeared in *The River Between*, were reprinted in Ngugi's *Secret Lives and Other Stories* (London: Heinemann, 1975).

4. He has described how he came to write this novel in a number of interviews: John de Villiers, "The Birth of a New East African Author," *Sunday Nation*, 3 May 1964, p. 10; *African Writers Talking: A Collection of Radio Interviews*, ed. Cosmo Pieterse and Dennis Duerden (London: Heinemann; New York: Africana Publishing Corp., 1972), pp. 12-22; and Reinhard Sander and Ian Munro, "'Tolstoy in Africa': An Interview with Ngugi wa Thiong'o," *Ba Shiru*, 5, 1 (1973). 21-30.

5. M. Karienye Yohanna, "There is More Than Politics in the Making of a Nation," *Kenya Weekly News*, 4 August 1961, p. 30.

6. Ibid.

7. Alan Marcuson et al. "James Ngugi Interviewed by Fellow Students at Leeds University, Alan Marcuson, Mike Gonzalez & Dave Williams," *Cultural Events in Africa*, 31 (1967), supp. i.

8. Pieterse and Duerden, p. 122.

9. "The Return," *Transition*, 3 (January 1962), 5-7; "The Martyr," *The New African*, 1, 6 (1962), 15-16, and 1, 7 (1962), 15-16.

10. "This Wound in My Heart" was first published in *Penpoint*, 13 (October 1962), 23-29, and then in Ngugi's *This Time Tomorrow* (Nairobi: East African Literature Bureau, n.d.) along with "The Rebels" and a radio play written and broadcast in England, "This Time Tomorrow." *The Black Hermit* did not appear in print until 1968 when it was published in London by Heinemann.

11. M. Karienye Yohanna, "The Black Hermit," *Kenya Weekly News*, 2 November 1962, p. 21.

12. Ngugi refers to himself as a "Junior Reporter" for the *Daily Nation* in the interview with Marcuson et al, p. ii. His journalistic essays for three Nairobi newspapers are listed in full in the bibliography attached,

so the footnotes that follow here will cite them only by date of publication.

13. 7 May 1961.

14. 4 June 1961.

15. 6 August 1961.

16. 13 August 1961.

17. 20 August 1961.

18. M. Karienye Yohanna, "'Stooge Writers," *Kenya Weekly News*, 23 March 1962, p. 21.

19. 27 May 1962.

20. 15 September 1963.

21. 5 August 1962. One also finds a reference in one of his essays (2 June 1963) to a man who returned home after the Emergency to find that his wife had had a child by another man; this appears to have been the person on whom Ngugi modeled his character Gikonyo in *A Grain of Wheat.*

22. 28 October 1962.

23. 6 August 1961.

24. 17 March 1963.

25. 22 April 1964.

26. 23 December 1962 ("Press").

27. 29 July 1962.

28. 1 July 1962; "A Kenyan at the Conference," *Transition*, 5 (1962), 7.

29. 2 December 1962.

30. 23 December 1962 ("Art").

31. 2 September 1962.

32. 23 December 1962 ("Art").

33. 2 September 1962; see also 19 July 1964.

34. 24 November 1963. Ngugi contributed a fuller review of this production to *Transition*, 12 (1964), 55.

35. Miriam Kahiga, "Ngugi on Language: For Literature that is National, not merely 'Afro-Saxon,'" *Daily Nation*, 24 July 1979, p. 13.

36. Marcuson et al, p. v.

37. 23 September 1962.

38. Kahiga, p. 13.

Bibliography of Ngugi wa Thiong'o's Early Journalism

1961

"'The African Personality' is a Delusion: Do Tigers have 'Tigritude'?" *Sunday Post*, 7 May 1961, p. 12.

"The New Voices: Some Emerging African Writers," *Sunday Post*, 4 June 1961, p. 11.

"African Culture: The Mistake That Kenyatta Made," *Sunday Post*, 6 August 1961, p. 10.

"The Nostalgia of 'Facing Mount Kenya,'" *Sunday Post*, 13 August 1961, p. 5.

"Some Problems of the New Villages," *Sunday Post*, 20 August 1961, p. 12.

1962

"Can the Educated African Meet This Challenge?" *Sunday Nation*, 27 May 1962, p. 31.

"The Future and the African Farmer," *Sunday Nation*, 3 June 1962, p. 33.

"Let's Get Out of the Dark and Take a Look at the Sun," *Sunday Nation*, 17 June 1962, p. 39.

"Adult Education Must Be Tackled," *Sunday Nation*, 24 June 1962, p. 43.

"Here are the Heralds of a New Awareness," *Sunday Nation*, 1 July 1962, p. 32.

"Let's See More School Integration," *Sunday Nation*, 8 July 1962, p. 25.

"There Must Be Freedom to Hear Opposite Points of View," *Sunday Nation*, 15 July 1962, p. 10.

"Why Not Let Us Be the Judges?" *Sunday Nation*, 29 July 1962, p. 4.

"Let Us Be Careful About What We Take from the Past," *Sunday Nation*, 5 August 1962, p. 31.

"Here's the Kenya I Want," *Sunday Nation*, 12 August 1962, p. 28.

"What Do We Really Mean by Neutralism?" *Sunday Nation*, 19 August 1962, p. 30.

"What is Happening about Federation?" *Sunday Nation*, 26 August 1962, p. 30.

"Must We Drag Africanness into Everything?" *Sunday Nation*, 2 September 1962, p. 30.

"What About Our Neighbours?" *Sunday Nation*, 9 September 1962, p. 31.

"How Much Rope Should Opponents Be Given?" *Sunday Nation*, 16 September 1962, p. 9.

"Swahili Must Have Its Rightful Place," *Sunday Nation*, 23 September 1962, p. 12.

"Why Don't These Two Leaders Learn from History?" *Sunday Nation*, 30 September 1962, p. 31.

"Our Women Must Be Allowed to Get Ahead Too," *Sunday Nation*, 7 October 1962, p. 12.

"Independence Needs a Degree of Trust," *Sunday Nation*, 14 October 1962, p. 11.

"We Must Halt Spread of 'Freedom Army,'" *Sunday Nation*, 28 October 1962, p. 31.

"Here's a Spirit Kenya Must Encourage," *Sunday Nation*, 4 November 1962, p. 22.

"African Writers Need a New Outlook," *Sunday Nation*, 2 December 1962, p. 29.

"All Praise to Obote but Kenya Must Help Itself," *Sunday Nation*, 9 December 1962, p. 35.

"Role of the Press," *Sunday Nation*, 23 December 1962, p. 6.

"Wanted—A Proper Place for Art," *Sunday Nation*, 23 December 1962, p. 11.

"Big Day for God's Children," *Sunday Nation*, 30 December 1962, p. 25.

1963

"I Say Kenya's Missionaries Failed Badly," *Sunday Nation*, 6 January 1963, p. 5.

"Co-operative Spirit is Not Enough," *Sunday Nation*, 3 February 1963, p. 4.

"Don't Forget Our Destination," *Sunday Nation*, 10 February 1963, pp. 12, 35.

"Even Brothers Can Cut Throats," *Sunday Nation*, 17 February 1963, p. 4.

"Respect Will Come When We Are Self-Sufficient," *Sunday Nation*, 17 March 1963, p. 29.

"The Oasis That is Makerere," *Sunday Nation*, 24 March 1963, p. 30.

"Perhaps It's a Case of Home Sweet Home," *Sunday Nation*, 7 April 1963, p. 10.

"Mboya is Right—Education is an Investment," *Sunday Nation*, 21 April 1963, pp. 10, 33.

"In the Old Days it was for the Old Men to Drink—Now Even Children Tread on the Toes of Their Fathers," *Sunday Nation*, 12 May 1963, p. 9.

"I Nodded in Sympathy, But Inwardly I was Groaning, for I Was No Use to Them," *Sunday Nation*, 26 May 1963, p. 5.

"A Change Has Come Over the Land—A Sense of Destiny Moves in Most People," *Sunday Nation*, 2 June 1963, p. 5.

"Now Let's See More Flexibility from University Colleges," *Sunday Nation*, 7 July 1963, p. 31.

"Isn't it Time the Public Were Asked about Federation?" *Sunday Nation*, 1 September 1963, p. 31.

"The Letter That Made My Heart Sink Inside Me," *Sunday Nation*, 15 September 1963, p. 15.

"Lack of Communication May be Barrier to an African United States," *Sunday Nation*, 22 September 1963, p. 14.

"It's Time We Broke Up This Tribal Outlook," *Sunday Nation*, 20 October 1963, p. 33.
"The Three Levels of Independence," *Sunday Nation*, 27 October 1963, p. 39.
"It's Time We Recognized That the Root-cause of Our Troubles May Lie in Us," *Sunday Nation*, 10 November 1963, p. 12.
"A New Mood Prevails," *Sunday Nation*, 24 November 1963, p. 14.
"Art Experiment Which Deserves to Succeed," *Sunday Nation*, 29 December 1963, p. 31.

1964

"The Negro is a Myth," *Daily Nation*, 9 April 1964, p. 6.
"Why Shakespeare in Africa?" *Daily Nation*, 22 April 1964, p. 6.
"African Socialism: Two Views," *Daily Nation*, 9 May 1964, p. 6.
"More is Needed from Educated Africans," *Sunday Nation*, 7 June 1964, p. 9.
"Humanism and African Socialism," *Daily Nation*, 12 June 1964, p. 6.
"Pensions—We Still Can't Rest Satisfied," *Sunday Nation*, 14 June 1964, p. 3.
"Teachers, Too, Want Cash!" *Sunday Nation*, 21 June 1964, p. 6.
"Thousands Flock to Volunteer for the Kenya Army," *Daily Nation*, 23 June 1964, pp. 8-9.
"How Do You Kill These Tribal Feelings?" *Sunday Nation*, 5 July 1964, p. 6.
"He's Africa's Poet-Statesman," *Daily Nation*, 10 July 1964, p. 6. [On Léopold Sédar Senghor.]
"What About the Workers?" *Sunday Nation*, 12 July 1964, p. 6.
"Commentary," *Daily Nation*, 17 July 1964, p. 6. [On need for better links between African countries.]
"I Hope THIS Theatre Group Won't Die, Too," *Sunday Nation*, 19 July 1964, pp. 6-7.
"Kenya Children Take to Ballet," *Daily Nation*, 23 July 1964, pp. 10-11.

"As President Nyerere Was Saying in 1960," *Sunday Nation*, 2 August 1964, p. 7.

"Commentary," *Daily Nation*, 4 August 1964, p. 6. [On importance of Pan-African students' conference opened at University College Nairobi.]

"Commentary," *Daily Nation*, 6 August 1964, p. 6. [On inadvisability of continued economic dependence on the European and American markets.]

"Commentary," *Daily Nation*, 7 August 1964, p. 6. [On American bombing raid on North Vietnamese torpedo bases in retaliation for attack on U.S. destroyer Maddox.]

"Commentary," *Daily Nation*, 8 August 1964, p. 6. [On Government's failure to give reasons for recent deportations, especially of Ian Henderson.]

"A Republic Before the End of the Year?" *Sunday Nation*, 9 August 1964, p. 6.

"Commentary," *Daily Nation*, 13 August 1964, p. 6. [On necessity that Government inform backbenchers of plans.]

"Commentary," *Daily Nation*, 14 August 1964, p. 6. [Applauds Government moves toward a federation.]

"Commentary," *Daily Nation*, 15 August 1964, p. 6. [On scrapping of regional powers in new constitution.]

"Now the Emphasis Must be on Co-ops," *Sunday Nation*, 16 August 1964, p. 6.

"Commentary," *Daily Nation*, 18 August 1964, p. 6. [On role of women in the development of the new Kenya.]

"Commentary," *Daily Nation*, 19 August 1964, p. 6. [On role of students in a developing country after independence.]

"Forget the Quitters, Remember the Desperate," *Sunday Nation*, 30 August 1964, p. 6.

Ngugi wa Thiong'o's Detention

The publication of Ngugi wa Thiong'o's fourth novel *Petals of Blood* in July 1977 was hailed as a major event in Kenya's young literary history. Ngugi, the country's best-known author, had not published a novel for ten years, and here at last was a blockbuster, his longest and most complex work of fiction. The book was formally launched at a public ceremony in Nairobi by Mwai Kibaki, then Minister of Finance and later Vice-President of Kenya, and soon officials in the Ministry of Education were talking about adopting it as a prescribed text for the "A"-level School Certificate Examination. Booksellers in Nairobi had difficulty keeping up with the demand for the novel, and Heinemann East Africa had to airfreight more copies from its London headquarters when supplies became depleted after only a few weeks. In short, *Petals of Blood* was a huge success, and the publicity surrounding its publication thrust Ngugi back into the national limelight. July 1977 was probably the supreme highpoint in his career as a writer.

But within six months Ngugi was in prison, having been detained by the Kenya Government for reasons that have never been publicly explained. He had been picked up in the early hours of December 31st when eleven police officers entered his home at Limuru saying that they wanted to interrogate him and to examine some of the books in his possession. After a two-hour search, the police took Ngugi to a police station in Kiambu about fifteen miles away, and his family and friends did not see him again until nearly twelve months later when he and other political detainees were released by Jomo Kenyatta's successor,

Daniel arap Moi, on Jamhuri Day (Independence Day, December 12th) in a gesture of national reconciliation.

Following their release most of the ex-detainees were reabsorbed into the mainstream of Kenyan society (several in fact won seats in Parliament in the next election), but Ngugi was not permitted to return to his position as Head of the Literature Department at the University of Nairobi. He applied for reinstatement, and students and faculty at the university made numerous appeals on his behalf to institutional and state authorities, but these efforts produced no tangible results. In 1982 Ngugi went to London at the invitation of his publisher, Heinemann Educational Books, to launch *Devil on the Cross,* a novel he had written during his detention. While he was away, some soldiers and civilians attempted to overthrow the Kenya Government. Since that time, Ngugi has lingered in Europe and America, reluctant to return to his homeland lest he be victimized again for his outspoken opposition to the current Kenyan regime. He thus remains today in another kind of prison, separated from friends and followers by the painful shackles of exile.

The questions about Ngugi's detention in Kenya that still need to be answered are (1) why was he detained, and (2) upon being released from detention, why was he prevented from resuming his position at the University of Nairobi? In the absence of official explanations from the Kenya Government, one can only speculate about such matters, but there are sufficient clues in the public record to suggest plausible answers to both questions. Let us look at the available evidence and try to interpret it.

What could have happened between July and December of 1977 to persuade people in power that Ngugi deserved to be put away? He had committed no known crimes, criminal or civil, so his offense must have been a political one, but what kind of political offense merits a penalty as severe as detention? Had Ngugi been plotting to overthrow the Government by force or take some other drastic treasonable action, he presumably would have been working in collusion with others, but since no one else was rounded up and incarcerated at the same time he was,[1] we must conclude that it was the Government's view that whatever he did, he did alone.

What had he done that no one else had done? Well, he had written that proletarian novel, *Petals of Blood*, which contained the harshest indictment of post-colonial Kenya that had ever appeared in local print, albeit in a fictional mode. The novel characterized the landowners and politicians in the country as greedy capitalist leeches living off the lifeblood of peasants and workers. And certain actions depicted in the narrative had an uncomfortably close correlation with real happenings, real settings, real people; here was recent Kenyan history being presented as a horror story about villainy in high places. Moreover, it was transparently clear that a portion of the verbal barrage was being aimed at prominent members of the Kenyatta family and that the Old Man himself was not wholly exempt from the mockery and criticism. This was powerful stuff indeed. Nearly all the reviews of the novel published in the Kenyan media spoke of it as an "explosive" book, a "bombshell"[2]—and with good reason. Ngugi had said some things that no one else had dared to say quite so openly. Had this been Uganda under Idi Amin, such outspokenness would have been rewarded with instant execution.

But this was Kenya, a more "democratic" society, where freedom of speech was still tolerated, or so it seemed. Ngugi himself, in an interview that appeared in Nairobi's *Sunday Nation* shortly after the novel was published,[3] said that he had no fears of getting in trouble with the authorities because of what he had written. He was only doing his job as a loyal citizen, a servant of his society:

> I do believe that criticism of our social institutions and structures is a very healthy thing for our society. I believe that we can move forward only through open and healthy criticisms. Writers must sincerely examine all aspects of our national life. If writers did not do this anywhere in the world, they would be failing in their duties.

Further, he insisted that the novel was more an attack on the nature of neocolonialism in a representative African nation than it was a critique of particular "grabbers of fruits" of independence in Kenya.

> It is very, very important for people to realize that it is not a question of one or two names...The novel tries to look at the structure of our society as the root of our social evils, rather than one or two individuals. It looks at things like social inequalities, what is at the root of unequal distribution of wealth, unemployment, etc....Even when talking about the so-called few Africans in top positions, this is not the issue really. The issue is having our own national life dominated by foreigners. Grabbing is a direct consequence of our economy being dominated by imperialism.

So Ngugi was writing another nationalistic novel, another assault on neocolonialism and imperialism, not merely a diatribe directed against the rich and powerful in Kenya. The real enemy was a foreign abstraction, not a local flesh-and-blood personage.

The novel nonetheless may have offended or disconcerted some of the ruling elite who perhaps felt that they had glimpsed unflattering reflections of themselves in it. But the novel alone did not lead to Ngugi's detention. Indeed, it has never been banned and is still freely available in Kenyan bookshops. Written words, especially those contained in literary works, do not seem to matter very much in Kenya. At least they have not yet been known to earn their authors a term in prison.

Spoken words, however, may have an altogether different resonance, particularly if they are spoken in one of Kenya's local languages. Ngugi appears to have been safe from harm so long as he continued writing his works in English. He first got into serious trouble when he co-authored a play in Kikuyu that was staged by villagers at the Kamirithu Community Educational and Cultural Centre in Limuru from October through November of 1977. After seven weeks of playing to full houses in an open-air theater that seated more than two thousand people, the production was closed down by the District Commissioner of the area who branded it "provocative" and "not to the best interest of the republic in general."[4] Forty days later Ngugi was picked up by the police for questioning, the first step towards his detention.

The play, entitled *Ngaahika Ndeenda* (I will marry when I want), was built around a triple theme of economic, religious and sexual exploitation. Kiguunda, a poor farm laborer, is persuaded by Kioi, his wealthy Christian employer, to sanctify his "sinful" traditional marriage in church. Kiguunda does not have enough money to pay for the expensive ceremony so he borrows some from Kioi's bank by offering his own one-and-a-half acres of farm land as collateral. When he defaults on the loan, the land is auctioned off and Kioi buys it so that he and a business associate can build an insecticide factory on it in partnership with a foreign firm. While this is going on, Kioi's playboy son seduces and impregnates Kiguunda's daughter and then rejects her. Kiguunda confronts Kioi on this issue, but Kioi denies that his son would have taken up with a "prostitute" and challenges Kiguunda to bring the matter to court so that "we shall see on whose side the law is."[5] Kiguunda responds by drawing his sword and threatening Kioi's life, a gesture that could be interpreted as symbolizing the successful armed revolt of the exploited masses against their bourgeois oppressors.

The play itself was not banned by the authorities. Rather, the District Commissioner revoked the Kamirithu Centre's licence to perform it. The play was published in Kikuyu by Heinemann East Africa in April 1980 and sold quite briskly, going through three printings (a total of 13,000 copies) in its first three months on the market. The Kenya Government has not attempted to prevent or discourage its publication or to interfere with its distribution to booksellers—facts that would seem to confirm the notion that oral performances speak louder than printed words in Kenya.

Why should a rural production of *Ngaahika Ndeenda* have been found so objectionable as to necessitate government suppression? After all, the play itself was not directly critical of the Government nor was it unpopular locally. Indeed, according to reports in the newspapers, this three-hour musical drama was an extraordinarily successful show, and people were coming from miles around to see it. Moreover, it was a community enterprise, almost a model *harambee* (self-help) project that involved a cross-section of the Limuru population—peasants, factory workers, petty traders, unemployed youths, university lecturers. It had originated as a scheme to promote and sustain literacy among villagers who had been taught to read and write at the Kamirithu Community Educational and Cultural Centre. Ngugi wa Mirii, who was supervising these literacy classes, and Ngugi wa Thiong'o, who was living in the community while teaching at the University of Nairobi, had been commissioned by the governing committee of the Centre to write a play that would give the new literates in the community something to do that would help them improve their recently acquired skills. The villagers actually collaborated in the development of the script, designed and built the open-air theatre, and raised the 75,000 shillings (about $10,000) necessary to produce the play.[6] From start to finish, the production was truly a communal undertaking.

What appears to have worried the authorities a bit was the play's immense popularity. Had it been a flop or fiasco, the government probably would not have bothered to intervene, preferring instead to allow this unusual theatrical experiment to die a quick, natural death. But the play was attracting hordes of viewers, the vast majority of whom were unrestrainedly enthusiastic about what they saw.

And it wasn't only the spectacle of a vibrant stage performance involving singing, dancing and drama that enthralled them; the message embedded in the play was getting across. Ngugi himself has said:

> I believe that the play, *Ngaahika Ndeenda*, was very popular because it talked about the extreme poverty of the people. I believe the play was popular because it talked about landlessness in our country. I believe the play was popular because it talked about the

> betrayal of the peasants and workers by the political "big-wigs." I believe the play was popular because it talked about the arrogance and the greed of the powerful and the wealthy. Again, I believe the play was popular because it depicted the true conditions of the rural people in the rural villages.[7]

If this is so, then it is not surprising that the District Commissioner of Kiambu received complaints about the performance from some members of the community who did not approve of what was being said and enacted on the Kamirithu stage. These complaints, supplemented by eyewitness reports from his officers, led the D.C. to decide to shut down the play, even though he himself had never seen a performance.

The reasons given by the Kiambu D.C. for taking this course of action are worth scrutinizing.[8] In elaborating his charge that the production was "provocative," the D.C. reiterated some of the complaints he had received that "the songs, dances and even the dialogue in the play were aimed at creating conflict between different classes of people in Kenya." He noted in particular that the term "homeguards" (Kamatimu) had been used frequently and that "such terms should not be used in public or elsewhere, since they could in the long run revive the bitterness of the Emergency period." Further, he felt that the play sought to "urge people to engage in a 'free-for-all' class war." He concluded his remarks by repeating that "the play does not put across the idea of reminding people to forget the past as our good government has been exhorting us."

These are far from trivial issues in the Kikuyu highlands, an area bloodied by very bitter fighting during the Mau Mau war. There are still many old wounds from that war that have not healed with time, many old scores that have never been settled. This play, the D.C. was saying, was reviving past animosities, reopening those wounds. The issue of "homeguards" was a particularly sensitive one, for this was the term applied to the Kikuyu who had fought in the war for independence on the side of the British colonial government. Some of these "homeguards" were portrayed in the play as among the worst of Kenya's neocolonial exploiters today, men who had profited handsomely from the national independence they had earlier sought to forestall, retard or subvert. The D.C. apparently feared that the play, by stirring up memories of the past, might lead to a disturbance of the peace, perhaps even to serious violence and mayhem. The revocation of the licence of the play may therefore be viewed as an effort to maintain law and order by suppressing a reawakening of the community's collective consciousness of history.

But the detention of Ngugi wa Thiong'o forty days later must be regarded as an act of another sort, especially since he was never charged with any crimes. It appears that he was victimized both as a penalty for his writings and as a warning to others who might be tempted by his example to mix too much politics with literature. Since no one else associated with *Ngaahika Ndeenda*—his co-author, the director, the actors—was detained, one must conclude that it was not the play alone that led to Ngugi's imprisonment; the play may have been the last straw but it was not the only straw in Ngugi's case. Also, since no charges were filed against him, it must be assumed that the Kenyan Government knew that it had no legal justification for denying him his freedom. The state was deliberately victimizing him for no valid reason. So while the closing down of the play may be seen as a preventive measure, the detention of Ngugi must be recognized as a terror tactic.

Ngugi's experiences after his release from detention in December 1978 tend to confirm suspicions that he was being singled out for harassment, but it remains difficult to identify his harassers. First there was an attempt in March 1979 to ruin his reputation as a responsible citizen. He and the co-author of *Ngaahika Ndeenda*, Ngugi wa Mirii, had gone to a small bar at Kamirithu Trading Centre on the evening of March 7th, and at 12:40 a.m. local police officers swooped in and arrested them for drinking after hours (i.e., after midnight). They were also charged with behaving in a disorderly manner at the police station while they were being booked; it was said that they had shouted, banged the police counter and cell doors, refused to be searched or to have their belts taken off, and tried to force officers on duty to release them and other prisoners. Both men were later released on bail pending a hearing.[9]

When the case was tried in court on April 27th, the two Ngugis denied all charges, claiming that they were picked up at about 11:30 p.m., not 12:40 a.m., and that they had never resisted arrest, used abusive language, or behaved in a disorderly manner. They then made several counter-charges, asserting that they had been beaten and kicked by the arresting officers, had been thrown like "a bag of salt" into the police vehicle, and had never at any time been told why they were being arrested, even though they had repeatedly demanded to know the charges. Ngugi wa Thiong'o went further and stated that he had been sober, having drunk only two bottles of beer during the day; he explained that since being released from detention, he had been living peacefully at home with his family, and on the few occasions when he went out, he was very careful to monitor his alcoholic intake because he had been receiving constant death threats on the telephone: "I have been receiving these threats, including three yesterday. This has forced me to restrict my movements, because I don't know who is behind these death threats." He therefore drank very little "because I must be in the position of knowing what is happening around me."[10] Ngugi's charges of physical brutality were supported by a doctor who had examined both defendants on March 8th and found them suffering from injuries which might have been caused by a blunt instrument such as a shoe or a boot.

The Kiambu senior resident magistrate who heard the case was of the opinion that there had been exaggerations by both the prosecution and the defense, but he acquitted the Ngugis of the drinks charge on a minor technicality (the bar was not licensed), cleared them of the ancillary charges of disorderly conduct, and reprimanded the police for using unnecessary force in the arrest.[11] Ngugi wa Thiong'o had successfully exonerated himself in court, but the ominous telephone death threats continued in the months that followed.

Who would make such threats? Powerful national or local political figures? Wealthy landowners and businessmen? Ex-homeguards? Cranks? Pranksters? Ngugi himself said he did not know, and it is still impossible to determine whether this sort of terror emanated from a source inside or outside the Kenya Government. One would like to think that Government officials would not use such tactics, but then how does one account for the trumped-up drinks charge? Who would have sent policemen in the middle of the night to arrest two sober adults at a Kamirithu bar? Whoever was responsible for their arrest must have had sufficient political power to influence the manner in which laws are enforced in the community. Not everyone has the authority to send cops out on a raid.

The campaign to get Ngugi reinstated in his job at the University of Nairobi began almost as soon as he was released from detention. Initially Ngugi himself did not take an active part in this campaign, preferring to wait to hear from the university. But when university officials remained silent on the matter, students began to hold mass meetings, make appeals to the administrative authorities, and send petitions directly to the Chancellor, who happened to be President Daniel arap Moi. Still nothing happened. After two and a half months had passed, Ngugi's faculty colleagues met and revived a quiescent University Academic Staff Union in order to exert pressure of their own. The Executive Committee of the Union met with the Vice-Chancellor and then the Union addressed its own petition to Chancellor Moi, urging that Ngugi be allowed to resume his teaching duties on the grounds that

> he is a patriot and a scholar who greatly loves his country; he is an outstanding teacher with proven capability to contribute to the development of our society; he is the only Kenyan creative writer of international repute...[and] he can only participate fully in nation-building by taking his place in the University.[12]

The Government's response to this petition took the form of complete silence. Another two and a half months passed. Finally Ngugi himself wrote to the University Council expressing his readiness to resume teaching duties. Following upon this, the Executive Committee of the Union met with the Vice-Chancellor early in June to discuss the case further, whereupon they were told that "the question of Prof. Ngugi rested with people other than the University authorities. His situation...was an 'act of state.'"[13]

During the next six weeks the faculty Union tried without success to arrange an appointment with President/Chancellor Moi. They also sent him another petition and issued a lengthy press release telling what had led to their petition. By the end of July, Members of Kenya's Parliament were beginning to ask the Assistant Minister of Education to explain why Ngugi was being denied the opportunity to resume his duties at the university. The Assistant Minister replied that Ngugi could resume his teaching career if he complied with his employer's wish that he reapply for his former position and meet certain conditions. The university authorities felt it was necessary for him to reapply because he had already been paid his terminal benefits when his contract had expired while he was in detention.[14] The Government, in other words, was shifting the blame for his non-reinstatement back to the university as well as onto Ngugi himself. It was merely a matter of completing all the bureaucratic paperwork, filling out the necessary forms.

But Ngugi didn't see it this way, and he was quick to point out the contradictions between the statements made by the Assistant Minister of Education and those contained in letters and remarks by university officials. First, he revealed that he had been paid terminal benefits on December 18, 1978, six days after he had been released from detention, not while he was in detention. Second, he pointed out that he was on "permanent and pensionable terms of service and not on contract" at the university; this meant that he should not have been dismissed except upon conviction for criminal activity, but during the many months he was in detention, he had never even been charged with committing a crime. Third, he had not been offered new terms of employment by the university. Moreover, only a few days after the Assistant Minister's statement, he had received a letter from the Registrar of the university reiterating the view that "the contract between yourself and the University of Nairobi was dissolved by an act of state the day you were taken away and detained." Ngugi had also been told this earlier by the Vice-Chancellor of the university, who had stated that his case was "a matter of public security and needed clearance from somewhere." When Ngugi had asked him to put this into writing, the Vice-Chancellor had told him that "nothing involving him and the university could be put in writing." Ngugi concluded that the university authorities, by making such statements and denying any responsibility for his dismissal, were "trying to imply that my case was beyond solution by any authority in Kenya." He characterized the dismissal itself as secret, unilateral, unjust, arbitrary and illegal.[15]

In the years since Ngugi made these charges, no progress has been made toward his reinstatement and none is likely to be made in the immediate future. In January 1980, the post of Professor in the Department of Literature at the University of Nairobi was publicly advertised, and Ngugi applied for it, but no action was taken on his application. In June 1980, Kenya's House of Parliament passed a motion urging the Government and the private sector "to assist the ex-detainees in obtaining the jobs for which they qualify to enable them to earn a living,"[16] but a month later President Moi responded by stating that he "could not be expected to give such people priority in jobs since they had been 'undermining' the government of the late President Jomo Kenyatta."[17] At the same time Moi accused the University Academic Staff Union of planning subversive activities, including killings, and took steps to have it banned.[18] Thus Ngugi lost the services of the one organized group in Kenya that was energetically lobbying in his behalf.

Ngugi's plight remains a national embarrassment today, but no one in the Kenya Government seems to be disposed to help him out. Soon he will have spent seventeen full years in exile, a form of detention without bars. Can Kenya afford to waste the talents of one of its most dedicated and highly principled sons? More important, can Kenya long continue to deny basic human rights to one of its citizens without suffering serious erosion of its credibility as a decent and just society? For Ngugi is the victim of an insidiously secretive form of repression—one that shows no official profile, presses no formal charges, answers no questions, honors no laws, respects no rights. Until the human face behind this invisible force can be identified and held accountable for perverting justice, Ngugi very likely will either remain in exile or suffer harassment and persecution when he returns home.

Kenya used to have a high reputation abroad not only for its stability and commitment to democratic ways but also for its moral integrity. In 1980 the United States Department of State published a report declaring that "Kenya's human rights record is among the best in Africa."[19] But if someone like Ngugi wa Thiong'o can be locked up for a year for no lawful reason, if he can be harassed afterwards by police authorities, if he can be prevented from returning to his job "without clearance from somewhere," if he can live safely only in exile, then Kenya does not deserve its reputation for social justice. Indeed, such deliberate victimization of individuals or groups is a sure sign of tyranny.

The most ominous aspect of Ngugi's situation is that he is not the only artist in Kenya to have suffered at the hands of the Government. Ngugi himself cited other examples in a 1980 BBC interview:

> The most important case was Abdilatif Abdullah, the well-known Swahili poet who was for three years put in a maximum security prison for writing a pamphlet saying "Kenya Twendapi?" (Kenya, where are we heading to?). Then in 1977...another writer and critic,

> Dr. Micere Mugo, was tortured in police cells. Much more recently in 1979, there was a case of some girls at a secondary school who wrote a play called "What a World, My People!" which was officially entered for a national drama competition. The play was performed in English to enthusiastic audiences but the moment they translated the play into Kikuyu and performed it for their peasant parents, the police moved in and stopped the performance of the play. Subsequently all the girls involved in writing the play or in acting in the play were expelled from the school. Let me put it this way: the girls were expelled from the school under one pretext or another, but it was very noticeable that all the girls expelled had been involved in the play. I am talking about a general tendency, since independence, for increasing repressive measures against writers and artists.[20]

What calls for such repressive measures? Why should the Government feel impelled to take such steps against writers and artists? Of his own case Ngugi has said: "I believe I was detained because I wrote truthfully about the Kenyan historical situation, both past and current."[21] This appears to have been the same offense that got Abdilatif Abdullah, Micere Mugo, and high school creators of "What a World, My People!" into trouble. Evidently, in Kenya today, "truth hurts," but it is most likely to hurt not those about whom it is spoken, nor those to whom it is spoken, but rather those patriots who dare to speak such truth aloud in a local language.

NOTES

1. Micere Githae-Mugo, then a Lecturer in the Department of Literature at the University of Nairobi, had been interrogated, physically abused by police, and held in prison for a few days early in 1978; no formal charges were ever brought against her and she was not detained. She co-authored a play with Ngugi wa Thiong'o, *The Trial of Dedan Kimathi* (Nairobi: Heinemann East Africa, 1976), which imaginatively reconstructed an episode in the life of Kenya's most famous Mau Mau leader. The play had been performed in Nairobi in October 1976 and had been one of two plays chosen to represent Kenya in the drama competition at the Second World Black and African Festival of Arts and Culture (FESTAC) held in Lagos in January and February of 1977.

2. See, e.g., *Weekly Review*, 27 June 1977, pp. 39-40; *Nairobi Times*, 6 November 1977, p. 11; *Viva*, July 1977, pp. 35-36; *Daily Nation*, 15 July 1977, p. 14.

3. *Sunday Nation*, 17 July 1977, p. 10.

4. Mungai wa Kamau, "Ngugi play banned because 'provocative,'" *Nairobi Times*, 4 December 1977, p. 1.

5. This summary is based on several reviews of the play: Karugu Gitau, *Weekly Review*, 9 January 1978, p. 13; Maguyu K. Maguyu, *Weekly Review*, 25 April 1980, pp. 47-48; Maguyu Maguyu, *Daily Nation*, 2 May 1980, p. 17.

6. For a brief history of the production, see *Weekly Review*, 9 January 1978, pp. 11-12; Ngugi wa Mirii, "Kamirithu Literacy Project," *Kenya Journal of Adult Education*, 7, 1 (1979), 7-10; Ngugi wa Thiong'o, "'For the first time, the people could see themselves,'" *Guardian*, 11 June 1980, p. 15; Miriam Kahiga, "Karimithu Revisited," *Daily Nation*, 19 January 1979, p. 11; and Ahmed Rajab, "Detained in Kenya," *Index on Censorship*, 7, 3 (1978), 7-10. Ngugi wa Thiong'o and Ngugi wa Mirii have also prefaced the published version of *Ngaahika Ndeenda* (Nairobi: Heinemann East Africa, 1980) with an account, in Kikuyu, of the production.

7. *Weekly Review*, 5 January 1979, p. 32.

8. See Mungai wa Kamau, p. 1, and Fibi Munene, "The Last Word," *Daily Nation*, 14 December 1977, p. 19.

9. *Standard*, 9 March 1979, p. 1; *Weekly Review*, 16 March 1979, pp. 21-22.

10. *Daily Nation*, 28 April 1979, p. 24.

11. *Daily Nation,* 5 May 1979, pp. 1, 24; *Weekly Review,* 11 May 1979, p. 23.

12. Quoted from "A Brief Report on USU's Struggle to Have Prof. Ngugi Resume His Duties at the University," mimeographed newsletter of the University Academic Staff Union (ca. May 1980), pp. 55-56.

13. *Weekly Review,* 20 July 1979, p. 13.

14. *Daily Nation,* 1 August 1979, p. 4; *Weekly Review,* 3 August 1979, pp. 5-6.

15. *Weekly Review,* 24 August 1979, p. 11; *Daily Nation,* 21 August 1979, p. 20; *Standard,* 21 August 1979, p. 2.

16. *Standard,* 12 June 1980, p. 2; *Sunday Nation,* 15 June 1980, p. 5.

17. *Weekly Review,* 11 July 1980, pp. 10-11.

18. *Weekly Review,* 18 July 1980, p. 4.

19. United States Department of State Bureau of Public Affairs, "Horn of Africa," *Current Policy,* No. 141 (25 February 1980), p. 3.

20. BBC African Service, *Arts and Africa,* No. 347G (1980), p. 1.

21. Ngugi wa Thiong'o, "The Making of a Rebel," *Index on Censorship,* 9, 3 (1980), 24.

Amos Tutuola's Search for a Publisher

The story of Amos Tutuola's surprising rise to literary fame has been told so often that it has almost gained the stature of a legend or modern-day myth.[1] We have Amos, the unpromising hero, setting out on an impossible quest (namely, publication in postwar London of a tall tale set in an African fantasy world and written in substandard English), yet after a series of accidents and unexpected happenings in lands remote from his experience, he manages to achieve his goal and win a substantial reward for his brave efforts. In this mythopoetic scenario Faber and Faber usually are cast in the role of the fairy godmother who rescues our hero from oblivion and sets him on the path to success, and Dylan Thomas appears as the godfather whose words of blessing help him along the way. The sheer pluck of the hero, the quixotic nature of his quest, and the benevolent intervention of sympathetic foreign spirits thus conspire to produce a miracle—Amos Tutuola, the unlettered man of letters.

If we examine this legend more closely, looking at the factual substance underlying the lore, we shall see that the story is more complicated than may be popularly supposed, and that it involves a wider cast of characters in leading and supporting roles. However, these additional facts, gleaned from the reminiscences of some of the dramatis personae, including Amos Tutuola, as well as from letters and documents that hitherto have been unavailable for public scrutiny, do not make the story any less fantastic. Indeed, it now appears all the more remarkable that Amos Tutuola happened to wind up in print. It took not just one lucky break to bring this about but a whole chain of fortuitous circumstances working almost magically to promote this pilgrim's progress.

The story begins in 1948, some months after Tutuola got married. He was then working as a messenger in the Department of Labour in Lagos, but his job left him with lots of free time on his hands, for there were not many messages to carry. A "Portrait" of Tutuola published in *West Africa* in 1954 notes that

> He was now for the first time conscious of the weight of hours. To free his mind from the boredom of clock-watching he reverted to an almost forgotten childhood habit of story-telling. But an office worker cannot very well tell stories through the spoken word, even with the indulgent employers Tutuola seems to have had, so he wrote them on scrap paper. Of his first written story, *The Wild Hunter in the Bush of Ghosts,* he says "in a day I cannot sit down doing nothing. I was just playing at it. My intention was not to send it to anywhere."[2]

Actually Tutuola's first story, "The Wild Hunter in the Bush of the Ghosts,"[3] had been composed in collaboration with one of his friends, Edward Akinbiyi, who also worked in the Department of Labour. In a letter Tutuola stated that "I was not the only person who wrote it but my frien [sic] and I joined hands together to write it."[4] The exact nature and extent of this creative collaboration are matters that have not yet been fully explored, but Tutuola certainly was the one who wrote out the final draft of the story, which came to 77 single-spaced foolscap pages. This he did after offering the story to a London publisher and receiving a reply indicating that they would indeed be interested in looking at the manuscript.

The publisher he had approached was not Faber and Faber but Focal Press, a publisher of technical books on photography. Tutuola, a keen amateur photographer who had set up a "photo-service" in Ebute-Metta with a view toward taking up photography "as a profession,"[5] owned a number of books by this publisher and found their London editorial address in one of them. When he wrote, he asked if Focal Press would like to consider a manuscript about spirits in the Nigerian bush illustrated with photographs of the spirits! This was an offer that no photography publisher could refuse. A. Kraszna-Krausz, Director of Focal Press, noted in a letter that "what I was really intrigued by when inviting Tutuola to submit his work was his claim to be able to photograph ghosts."[6] When the manuscript arrived a few months later, there were sixteen photographic negatives accompanying it, most of which, when developed, turned out to be snapshots of hand-drawn sketches of spirits featured in the story. There was also one photograph of a human being. Tutuola had hired a schoolboy to draw the sketches and then had photographed what the boy had drawn.

A reputable publisher of technical books on photography obviously could not offer to print such a bizarre narrative as "The Wild Hunter in the Bush of the Ghosts," but Kraszna-Krausz, impressed by the amount of labor that had gone into writing out the story in longhand, felt the author deserved some compensation for his efforts and therefore bought the manuscript for a nominal sum. He had absolutely no intention of publishing it and believed no other publisher in London would seriously consider bringing out such a book. He himself was interested in it only as a curiosity and conversation piece.[7]

The tale closely resembles Tutuola's six published narratives but also contains a few notable idiosyncrasies that make it unique. Like the others, it is an episodic adventure story told in the first person by a hero who has been forced to undertake a long, hazardous journey in a spirit-haunted wilderness. As he wanders from one "town" to another in this ghostly forest seeking a way home, he encounters strange creatures and experiences extreme deprivations, tortures and other "punishments" that test his mettle and ingenuity. Fortunately, a generous legacy of protective medicine (in this case, the "juju" of his father, a famous hunter and magician) enables him to survive any ordeals he fails to avoid through cunning or chance. After decades of such exploits, which include visits to both heaven and hell, the Wild Hunter finally returns to the human world and offers his people the benefits of his knowledge of other realms.

Anyone familiar with Tutuola's other works will recognize in this brief synopsis a number of features that place "The Wild Hunter in the Bush of the Ghosts" in the same distinctive narrative tradition. First there is the monomythic cyclical structure of the story, involving a Departure, an Initiation and a Return.[8] Then there is the loosely coordinated internal structure which is the result of a concatenation of fictive units strung together on the lifeline of a fabulous hero in an almost random order. The hero himself is a composite of the most popular folklore protagonists—hunter, magician, trickster, superman, culture hero—and some of the adventures he relates closely resemble episodes in well-known Yoruba yarns (e.g., a half-bodied ghost, similar to the half-bodied child found not only in folktales but also in Tutuola's *The Palm-Wine Drinkard,* torments the Wild Hunter before he gets to the Fifth Town of Ghosts[9]). Moreover, certain motifs such as the facile shifting of bodily shapes, the contests between rival magicians, and the enounters with monsters, mutants, and multiform ghosts clearly derive from oral tradition. The story is a collage of borrowed materials put together in an eclectic manner by a resourceful raconteur working well within the conventions governing oral storytelling.

Yet there are signs of literary influence too. The narrative frame—a hunter's memoirs prefaced by a brief biography of the hunter's father—appears to have been inspired by D. O. Fagunwa's *Ogboju ode ninu igbo irunmale,*[10] which uses the same device. Indeed, the very title of Tutuola's story "The Wild Hunter in the Bush of Ghosts" is extremely close to Fagunwa's "The Brave Hunter in the Forest of Four Hundred Spirits" (a literal translation of *Ogboju ode...*), suggesting a strong kindred relationship between the texts possibly bordering on illegitimacy. In any case, no one could deny that they belong to the same family of letters. Moreover, there is sufficient internal evidence to suggest a genetic connection between Tutuola's tale and Bunyan's *Pilgrim's Progress,* but it is possible that some of these Christian chromosomes may have been passed on to Tutuola via Fagunwa.

Tutuola was greatly encouraged by Focal Press's invitation to submit his manuscript for consideration. Immediately after completing "The Wild Hunter..." and sending it off, he sat down and started writing another tale like it, a tale he decided to call "The Palm-Wine Drinker and His Dead Palm-Wine Tapster in the Deads' Town."[11] This one he wrote on his own, though he admits having borrowed a number of motifs from an old story-teller he used to visit at a nearby palm plantation on Sunday afternoons.[12] A careful reader of *The Palm-Wine Drinkard* will find in it two references to the earlier narrative which Tutuola apparently assumed was going to be published by Focal Press.[13]

Before Tutuola completed "The Palm-Wine Drinker," however, he may have learned that Focal Press would not be able to publish "The Wild Hunter...", for when he was ready to send off the second manuscript, he began to search for another outlet for publication. It was at this time that he came across an advertisement in an issue of *Nigeria Magazine* listing new books by African authors published by Lutterworth Press, a London-based company founded by the United Society for Christian Literature.[14] He wrote to the Lutterworth Press on 31 January 1950, asking if they would be willing to publish his new manuscript. His lack of familiarity with standard publishing procedures must have been evident in his letter, for a reply on March 10th by Mary Senior, "Assistant Secretary (Africa)" of the United Society for Christian Literature, reads:

> I am afraid you do not understand the way in which publishers do business. An author submits a manuscript to a publisher who reads or has it read. Judging by the report he then considers whether it is possible to accept the manuscript for publication. If acceptable it is at this stage that terms are negotiated.
>
> If you have a manuscript which you would care to submit to us we will gladly read it and advise you.[15]

Upon receiving this letter, Amos Tutuola promptly dispatched the manuscript of "The Palm-Wine Drinker" to U.S.C.L./ Lutterworth Press in London.

In a letter written eighteen years later Mary Senior recalled what happened when the manuscript arrived:

> Mr. Tutuola addressed his manuscript to the United Society for Christian Literature...As I was then Africa Editorial Secretary it came straight to me and I was the first to read it. I sent the MS to the late Rev. T. Cullen Young, a former Secretary of the Society, who had initiated the Society's policy of encouragement to African authors and he confirmed my judgement saying, if I remember rightly, that I should never see anything like it again. For reasons domestic to the Society I was unable to get it included in our publishing programme, though I tried to do so, (I am not sure but we had probably not come through the aftermath of the war; publishing was extremely difficult and [there was] a limited supply of paper till some time after the war; I forget the date when things became easier.) When finally the verdict went that we could not include it in our publishing programme I wrote to that effect to Mr. Tutuola...and offered to do my best to find a publisher.[16]

Her letter to Tutuola dated 23 October 1950, states:

> We have been very interested indeed in your manuscript and the readers to whom we have shown it have commended it highly. To our great regret we are ourselves unable to find a place for it in our publishing programme. I have, however, been doing my best to interest other publishers in it, one of whom has to-day asked to see the manuscript. If they should be interested in publication I expect you will hear from them direct. If not I will go on trying to get someone to take it up.[17]

The publisher to whom Mary Senior sent the manuscript in October was Thomas Nelson and Sons, where a friend of hers, Jonathan Curling, worked as Publicity Manager. According to Jocelyn Oliver, the Book Editor at Lutterworth Press, Curling was "enormously impressed" with the manuscript, but when he presented it to the Overseas Director of the company suggesting that it be considered for publication, he was told,

"Don't be silly!",[18] and the manuscript was returned to Lutterworth Press on 19 February 1951.[19]

It is at this point that Jocelyn Oliver played a crucial role in determining the fate of "The Palm-Wine Drinker." To recount the story in his own words:

> [Mary] Senior realized she had got hold of something pretty extraordinary, though her interest was ethnological rather than literary, and she took the MS to Martin Lewis, then General Manager of the U.S.C.L./Lutterworth Press. An excellent business manager, he had not the flair...to say much more than that Tutuola must be off his head—and if Miss Senior really expected him to publish it, she must be off hers. Piqued, she showed the MS. to me. I said that Tutuola might well be off his head, for here was clearly the one work of undoubted genius I had come across in my (then) twenty years of book-editing. I asked her permission to send it [to] Richard de la Mare, of Faber, he being the one man I knew who would not only also recognize it for what it was, but had the power and might have the courage to publish it. He had, as you know—where-upon I fade from the scene...
>
> I had no personal contact with Tutuola whatever. But I am proud and delighted to have been responsible for the Drinkard's birth in print. Whoever sent the MS. about would never have thought of Faber and Faber, and I am still doubtful whether anyone else would have dared to handle what, by all the rules of commerce...ought to have turned out a costly flop.[20]
>
> Mary Senior's was a nobler aim than mine: she cared passionately for the MS. as a remarkable piece of work by an *African*. I didn't care whether the writer was African or Chinese: it was as a *literary* work that I felt something must be done about it.[21]

Oliver's letter to Richard de la Mare, dated the same day the manuscript had been returned to Lutterworth Press from Thomas Nelson and Sons, reads:

> Do you think Mr. Eliot would have time to look at the enclosed MS. which has been sent to us from Africa?

> Lutterworth funks it, I'm sorry to say; but *if* it is original it is the one work of real genius that has come my way in twenty-five years' publishing! I hate to think of its blushing unseen.[22]

The "Mr. Eliot" Oliver refers to was of course T.S. Eliot, then a Senior Editor at Faber and Faber. There is no documentary evidence available to indicate what Eliot's reaction to the manuscript was, but the Book Committee at Faber and Faber that initially considered it may have wanted to check up on one clause in Oliver's letter ("*if* it is original...") for on March 15, Geoffrey Faber himself wrote a letter of inquiry to Daryll Forde, a renowned Africanist teaching in the Department of Anthropology at University College, London:

> My dear Daryll,
> I wonder if I can bother you again. We have had submitted to us a highly unusual MS. about which we are anxious to get a line from an anthropologist familiar with the workings of the West African imagination; and I am writing to ask if you can help me over this—whether yourself or by an introduction to somebody else. It is a long rambling ghost, spook and juju story by a West African native. It bears the title *The Palm-Wine Drinker and His Dead Palm-Wine Tapster in the Deads-Town*. It is told in intelligible though hardly idiomatic English, at any rate the idioms are not English idioms! It is full of the most extraordinary horrors, some of them very funny indeed; but always there is a disturbing hint of terror which makes the comicalities look not so comic after all. We think it possible that it might conceivably have something of a success if published here. But we should like to know whether it has its roots in the common West African mind.
>
> It is written in longhand, but easily legible. We don't know the name of the author, or even what part of Africa he comes from—I have taken the "West African" provenance from one of our readers reports; so I suppose there is some internal evidence about that. The manuscript has been sent on to us by a smaller publishing firm, and I dare say we could track the author down through them. I should be most grateful if you could help us at all.[23]

Forde replied a few days later, suggesting that the best person to read the manuscript would be S.O. Biobaku, a postgraduate historian originally from Abeokuta and Ibadan but now living in London.[24] The manuscript presumably was sent to Biobaku, and Biobaku presumably affirmed its authenticity, for on 31 May Ann Faber wrote to Jocelyn Oliver:

> The Book Committee has asked me to write to you about a manuscript which you sent us in February, "The Palm Wine Drinker," from Africa. We have talked backwards and forwards about this story and have taken some trouble to discover whether it is likely to be genuine. We think it is and we are keen to take a chance with it. I wonder whether you could now put me in touch with the author and whether you have any other information which is likely to be useful?[25]

Oliver had left U.S.C.L./Lutterworth Press by then, but Mary Senior responded the next day, providing Tutuola's address in Lagos and quoting from a letter from Tutuola that had accompanied the manuscript when originally submitted to U.S.C.L./Lutterworth Press. Tutuola apparently had included some drawings to illustrate the story, just as he had when submitting "The Wild Hunter In the Bush of the Ghosts" to Focal Press. Here is what he had said about his manuscript:

> I shall be very much grateful if you will correct my "WRONG-ENGLISH" etc. and can alter the story itself if possible, of course, it is not necessary to tell you as you are an expert in this work.
>
> You will see all the pictures numbered (9 pictures) and you will understand what I wanted to draw as all of these (pictures) are only rough drawings, but however, I want you to improve them better as how it will attract the buyers of the story when published out for sale.
>
> In conclusion, I leave everything for you to do as you can in such a way that it will pay for both of us.[26]

On 21 June 1951, Alan Pringle of Faber and Faber wrote the following letter to Amos Tutuola, offering him a contract for the book:

> We have read with great interest your MS., *The Palm Wine Drinker*, which was forwarded to us by the Lutterworth Press, and we find ourselves very keen to publish it.
>
> The Lutterworth Press have sent us passages from your letter to them about the question of editing the text, and about illustrations. To take the second point first, we have considered whether we might have your rough drawings redrawn but are of the opinion that the story should be left to speak for itself, without illustrations of any kind.
>
> About the text—we agree that your English is not always conventional English as written in this country, but for that very reason we think it would be a great pity to make it conform to all the rules of grammar and spelling. Just as no one but a West African could have had such a strange tale to tell, so your manner of writing it has a charm of its own. We propose therefore that our reader should go through the manuscript before it is set up in type, correcting what are evidently copying errors, accidental omissions, confusions or inconsistencies, but leaving intact all those expressions which, though strictly speaking erroneous, are more graphic than the correct expressions would be. You can depend upon it that we have the success of the book at heart, and we hope you will be content to leave the matter to our judgement.
>
> Perhaps you would let me know, when you write, if you would wish us to send printer's proofs to you in case you have any corrections to make; if so, it would be important that your corrections should then be as few and as small as possible, owing to the expense of shifting type.
>
> The terms we suggest are an advance of £25, payable on publication, on account of a royalty of ten per cent. of the published price on all copies sold. The published price would be 10s 6d net. We should like to have the option of publishing your next book on terms to be mutually agreed.
>
> If you would let me know that these terms are acceptable to yourself, we would have a contract drawn up for signature.[27]

Tutuola was quick to reply. On 27 June. he wrote Pringle:

> Thank you for your letter of June 21st. I am very glad to read in your letter that you will publish the M/S and also the letter points out about the correction of my wrong English etc., in conclusion, I leave everything for you to do as how it will profit for both of us, and is no need of sending me the printer's proofs for corrections as you are an expert in this field.
>
> 2. All the terms are accepted but I suggest that this 10% is too poor and it would be better if it is 20% or 25%, but this does not debar you to start work. I leave all for you to judge.
>
> 3. Please, will you explain in full a paragraph of your letter which reads as follows:—"We should like to have the option of publishing your 'NEXT BOOK' on terms to be mutually agreed."
>
> Awaiting your early reply, please.
>
> Yours truly,
>
> A. TUTUOLA
>
> N.B. Paragraphs 2 and 3 above are not debar you in any way to start the work.[28]

Pringle was away on holiday when Tutuola's letter arrived, but Faber and Faber's Book Committee went ahead and approved an improvement in the terms of Tutuola's contract so that Pringle could respond as follows on July 16th:

> Thank you for your letter of June 27th, from which I am glad to learn that we may go ahead with the preparation of your manuscript for the printer and with the typesetting itself. I am now enclosing a copy of the contract which we have drawn up, and should be grateful if you would sign at the end and initial the first two sheets at the foot. If you would then return it to us we would send you a copy signed by ourselves.
>
> You will see from clause 6(a) that we have responded to your request by increasing the royalties to 10% on the first 3,000 copies sold, 12% on copies sold between 3000 and 6000, and 15% thereafter.
>
> The meaning of the option clause is that should you write another book after your first, and consider publishing it, you undertake to give us an opportunity of making you an offer for

> publication before any other publisher. It is our normal practice to ask for this.[29]

Again Tutuola replied immediately, this time revealing that he would soon send Faber and Faber another story he was writing.

> Thank you for you letter of 16th July, 1951, in which you enclosed the "AGREEMENT" which I read carefully and agreed as how it is made before initialled the first two sheets and also signed my signature in full on the third sheet.
>
> Now I do understand what you mean in paragraph 5 of your letter of June, 21st, and I have agreed for it in paragraph 8 of the Agreement.
>
> Please, I shall be expecting your reply very early as I am now preparing to travel very soon, but I will not keep long before I will return and will let you know as soon as I come back, of course, this does not disturb you to write me at any time you like and my address still remains as above.
>
> The title of another story which will follow "The Palm Wine Drinker" is "MY LIFE IN THE BUSH OF GHOSTS" the bush which I entered since I was 7 years old, there I met my dead cousin who established Christianity, etc. works in the 10th town of ghosts. I married a "Superlady" in the church of Evils and my best man is a ghost who is always seeking evil things to do and some of the prominent ghosts as—Smelling ghost, triplicated ghost, Eye flashed mother, the ruler of the 8th town of Short ghosts, Television handed ghostess" etc. But this will be more in volume than the "Palm Wine Drinker" and will be typed before sent to you whenever you ask for it.
>
> Please if you do not use the rough drawings which I sent together with the "Palm wine Drinker" will you send it by surface mail to me.[30]

Faber and Faber were not certain that they wanted to risk publishing a second book by Tutuola but they were willing to consider the possibility if *The Palm-Wine Drinker* caught on. On 3 August, Pringle wrote to Tutuola:

> Many thanks for your letter of July 20th from which we were glad to learn that you propose to follow up THE PALM WINE DRINKER with another volume called MY LIFE IN THE BUSH OF GHOSTS. I am not quite clear from your letter whether the book is complete except for the typing. We should certainly be pleased to read it as soon as you like, although it might be that we should wish to postpone a decision on the second book until we had published THE PALM WINE DRINKER and seen its reception. Therefore, if you care to send us MY LIFE IN THE BUSH OF GHOSTS soon, we shall certainly read it, but not necessarily be able to give you a decision for some time; if you would prefer not to have the second book typed until the first had been published, we should quite understand.
>
> We returned the rough drawings for THE PALM WINE DRINKER on July the 18th.
>
> With this letter we are enclosing the contract for the PALM WINE DRINKER which has been signed by our Chairman. This is the copy you keep.[31]

In response to Pringle's letter, Tutuola on 27 August tried to clarify a few points about "My Life in the Bush of Ghosts" and also raised a new matter concerning a possible Yoruba translation of "The Palm Wine Drinker."

> I apologize in delaying to reply your letters of 3rd August 1951, in which you enclosed my own copy of the Agreement and of 17th July, with the rough drawings for "Palm Wine Drinker." This is to acknowledge them with many thanks.
>
> I am very glad too to read in your last letter of 3rd August, which I met at home when returned from tour, that you like to see the M/S of "My Life in the Bush of Ghosts." The letter is also points out that no any decision will be given at present. Yes I am agree for that and also very glad to tell you that it has been completed for long time and you will understand it more than the way that I wrote the P.W.D. but as this one is more interested and more in volume than the P.W.D., so therefore I should like to have it typed clearly before sent to you as I do not worry as long as it can remain with you, and I am very sorry to tell you that I given it to many

> typists for typing but when every one of them charged heavy amount which I cannot pay at present, then I keep it until I would get such amount to pay for one who would type it and then send it to you by ordinary mail. But I am quite sure that if you go through this "My Life in the Bush of Ghosts," you will like to publish it earlier then the time you expected to publish it before, as it is very interested more than the "P.W.D."
>
> "HINT" - This is to inform you that I received an official letter (25.8.51) from the Deputy Director of Education (Nigeria) that he should be very glad if I would send the M/S of P.W.D. in "YORUBA" language for consideration to be published for the schools as a "YORUBA" literature book and also for the interest of the other people. This is why I wrote to you to send the rough drawings which I just received.
>
> But if the Deputy Director of Education (Nigeria) considers it for publication, I am quite sure it would be published in U.K. by a publisher of educational books and according to the "Clause 8" of our Agreement I would inform the publisher when it is time, to deal with you direct and not to me.
>
> To publish P.W.D. in "YORUBA" language (My language) does not affect the one that published in English etc., in any way as there would be no single word to be used in it in English as it is only for those who cannot read English.
>
> I shall be very glad if you will I pay immediate attention to paragraph 2 and to reply very early.[32]

This time Tutuola did not receive a prompt reply, so on 3 October he wrote a follow-up note raising the translation issue again and requesting immediate payment of his £25 advance for "The Palm-Wine Drinker" which was not due until publication of the book.

> This is to remind you about the paragraph 3 of my letter dated 27th August, 1951, to which reply has not been received since then. I shall be very glad if you will let me hear about it very urgent, because I have received more than two letters from the Deputy Director of Education about the M/S (M/S in Yoruba), and as you are aware that I ought to spend some amount on it before submitted and also on "My Life in the Bush of Ghosts" which has been

> completed, therefore I shall be very glad if you will send the advance of £25 as stated in the Agreement together with the reply of this letter.
>
> Many thanks for your urgent reply.[33]

The Book Committee at Faber and Faber once again yielded to Tutuola's request, and Pringle conveyed the message to him in a letter dated October 11th:

> Thank you for your letter of October 3rd. I am sorry that we did not reply to the third paragraph of your letter of August 27th about the proposal from the Deputy Director of Education in Nigeria that you should send the MS. of THE PALM WINE DRINKER in the Yoruba language for consideration as a school text book and work of Yoruba literature. I thought the Manager would be replying to this point, and he thought that I was doing so.
>
> However, we are certainly very glad that this opportunity has presented itself, and we think it a very good plan that you should follow it up.
>
> In view of what you say, we agree to pay now the twenty-five pounds advance which, by the terms of the contract for THE PALM WINE DRINKER, was to be payable on publication, and we are making arrangements for payment to be made immediately.[34]

Unfortunately, when the sum was transmitted through Faber and Faber's banker's agents in Lagos a few days later, a British income tax levied at the rate of 9/6d on the £ had reduced it to a total of £13.2s.6d. When Tutuola complained that "the income tax of your country is too much and is a great loss" and should not be deducted from his royalties because he was also paying income tax in Nigeria,[35] Faber and Faber looked into the matter and discovered that though national income tax regulations required them "to deduct British Income Tax at the standard rate...from all payments for royalties made to authors resident outside the United Kingdom," a special agreement between Nigeria and Britain made it "possible for payments to be made without taxation being levied in both countries."[36] So forms were sent to

Tutuola enabling him to file exemption from British income tax deductions.

Reading through this mass of correspondence, one cannot fail to be impressed with the justness and generosity of Faber and Faber's dealings with Tutuola. They were aware that he was a special kind of author and they were careful to accord him special treatment. When he made unusual requests, such as asking them to check on prices of cameras in London for him, or later ordering books or equipment through them payable out of his royalties, Alan Pringle always tried to supply what was needed and keep the records of such transactions straight. There is no evidence of any attempt on the part of Faber and Faber to shortchange Tutuola or to cheat him out of what he had earned; this must be stated unequivocally for there have been a number of emotional but unsubstantiated allegations made—and printed![37]—about such matters in the past. It is clear from their correspondence with him that Faber and Faber's relationship with Tutuola has always been entirely honorable.

As an example of one of Tutuola's special requests, here is his letter of 21 March 1952, written six weeks before *The Palm-Wine Drinkard* was published on 2 May. The letter is not written in Tutuola's usual style so we may assume that he hired a professional letter writer to draft it for him:

> I am really sorry to bore you with correspondence, but I have a problem which I wish to bring before you for sympathetic consideration. I am to enquire whether it could be possible to grant me a small loan of £30 to further my studies in a Private Institution overseas, having as a security the royalty which may be due to me in consequence of my humble work.
>
> I take no advantage of our business commitments to make this humble demand, but wish to lay hand on any avenue which may open its way to making me a better man in life.
>
> I shall be very grateful if you will consider my humble request and advise me by return post your decision.

> Thank you for my help in the matter.
> I am,
> Yours faithfully,
> Amos Tutuola[38]

This request was granted without hesitation, as were numerous others in the years that followed.

In the months before *The Palm-Wine Drinkard* was published, there was not only considerable enthusiasm at Faber and Faber about launching this singular book but also some curiosity about how reviewers and literary critics would respond to it. Portions of other letters and inhouse memos concerning Tutuola are worth quoting here because they reflect the attitude of his publishers to his work. For instance, on 13 July 1951, not long after the decision to publish had been made, Richard de la Mare wrote to Jocelyn Oliver:

> It seemed to me and to many of us to be a terrifying but quite fascinating book and we felt that we oughtn't to let it slip. What the reviewers will say about it I cannot imagine, but it will be more than interesting to see how they take it. It is many a long day since I have looked forward to the press for a book more than for this one!
>
> I want to thank you again for passing the ms. on to me—and I think you flattered us in doing so! I am so glad that we haven't disappointed you in your trust![39]

A few days later de la Mare reiterated:

> We all of us here have an odd excitement about this book, so there won't be more delay about its publication than can be helped.[40]

By September of the same year Faber and Faber were already looking for an American co-publisher for the book, though they were not pushing it very hard. When Pantheon Books expressed an interest in considering it, Peter du Sautoy responded:

> THE PALM WINE DRINKER by Amos Tutuola...is indeed a long shot and you probably won't want it in the end. However, by all means ask Herbert Read about it. He might even write an introduction for you, although so far as our edition goes we have decided to let it burst upon an astonished world unheralded and unrecommended.[41]

When Pantheon Books later asked to see "a carbon of the manuscript" or "the galleys when they are available"[42] du Sautoy wrote:

> THE PALM WINE DRINKER is now called THE PALM WINE DRINKARD, Drinkard being one of the original words invented by the remarkable author. We are really rather excited about this book. We hope that it may be possible to get a jacket designed by Harry Moore, but I am not sure if this has yet been arranged. I have no proofs to send you at present, but as soon as I have them they will be sent across at once. I do hope that you will find the book as exciting as we do. The manuscript was literally a manuscript, written by the author in long-hand, so there was no question of a carbon to show you.[43]

Pantheon received the proofs in March 1952 but found the book disappointing and rejected it, believing it would not be likely to attract American readers.[44] However, a few weeks later Faber and Faber's Spring and Summer catalogue had started circulating, and inquiries about the book were received in the following months from McGraw-Hill, Prentice-Hall, Random House, Norton, Noonday, William Morrow and the Book Find Club in New York City. Nearly all of these publishers read the book after publication and turned it down. An editor at Norton, for example, explained:

> Although I am afraid our decision is against an offer of publication in this country, I did want to write you and tell you, for what it is worth, that it is the sort of book that fascinates me. Since you published it, I suspect that you and I have something of the same

> weaknesses. It is *almost* that fascinating sort of off-the-trail book coming from an off-the-trail mind that sometimes catches the public eye, but the trouble as I see it lies in the word "almost." I am afraid Mr. Tutuola doesn't quite pull it off, and when the book is finished it isn't quite worth the confusion.
>
> I hope that I am speaking from just the American market point of view and that the book is a great success in England.[45]

To this du Sautoy replied:

> It is extremely good of you to have written about the book, instead of leaving us simply with a formal rejection. We do, of course, realize that it is not quite as good as it ought to be, but it is the unsophisticated product of a West African mind and we felt there was nothing to be done about it except leave it alone. When I say unsophisticated, that is not altogether true, since Tutuola has been to some extent influenced by at any rate the externals of Western civilization. It seemed to us to be an interesting example of genuine African writing and worth while publishing on that account. Its interest is possibly more anthropological than literary, but, apart from being in the end a little tedious, it has got a certain quality as a piece of unusual writing.
>
> The book has had a curious and not altogether intelligent reception here. That is not really surprising, since it is so far removed from the ordinary publications of to-day.[46]

Perhaps it was this "curious and not altogether intelligent reception" in England that made Faber and Faber a bit reluctant to make a commitment to Tutuola to publish "My Life in the Bush of Ghosts." The typescript of this narrative had been received late in January or early in February of 1952,[47] but it was not until about fifteen months later—nearly a full year after *The Palm-Wine Drinkard* had been published—that they offered Tutuola a contract for it.[48] And this they did only after having the story evaluated by two anthropologists—Mary Danielli and Geoffrey Parrinder—both of whom recommended it but for different reasons.[49] Perhaps what had initially given Faber and

Faber pause was the first reader's report they had received, which had come from a member of their own editorial board. Here is the entire text of that program as it was written by Thomas Stearns Eliot:

> I am rather apprehensive of Mr. Tutuola's turning out a Problem Child. He promises a sequel to this tale, namely his visit to the SECRET SOCIETY OF GHOSTS. However popular the PALMWINE DRINKARD may prove, I fear that the public appetite for this line of fiction may be satisfied with one book (One would not have wanted a series of successors to *The Young Visiters*).[50] I think that this one is worth publishing; but will the author go on being interesting to any but students of social psychology, and, on a deeper level, students of Colonial Policy?
>
> Not there are not just as good things here as in THE PALM WINE DRINKARD. Particularly appreciable is the correspondence exchange between the King of the Ghosts and The Flash Eyed Mother ("with reference to your undated letter No. 66/88"). But I found that my attention did sometimes wander and my interest flag during the interminable journeys from one Ghost Town to another. The beginning, however, is thrilling.[51]

Eliot's report, dated "Quinquagesima 1952" (i.e., the Sunday before Lent, or 24 February 1952), was not really a whole-hearted endorsement of "My Life in the Bush of Ghosts," and after consulting it, the Book Committee at Faber and Faber, like Prufrock, may have remained in a quandary of indecision, wondering "Do we dare? Do we dare?" *The Palm-Wine Drinkard* first had to prove itself, not only by winning encomiums from other prominent literary figures such as Dylan Thomas, Naomi Mitchison, V. S. Pritchett, Elspeth Huxley and Herbert Read, but also by selling enough copies on the open market to justify a publisher's confidence in the commercial possibilities of a sequel. It is perhaps significant that the decision to publish "My Life in the Bush of Ghosts" came not long after George Braziller had bought the American rights to *The Palm-Wine Drinkard* for his newly formed Book Find Club[52] and then had quickly resold them to Grove Press, who were very eager to publish more material by Tutuola and were pressing Faber and Faber to send them a copy of the typescript of "My Life in the Bush of Ghosts."[53] But this is another chapter in the saga of Tutuola's transmutation into print, a chapter that takes place in another strange land and that ought to be recounted in detail at another time.

Let us end here, as most modern imaginative works do, with a list of credits flashed on the screen acknowledging the contributions made by individuals and groups to the drama just enacted. Major roles were played by A. Kraszna-Krausz, Mary Senior, Jocelyn Oliver, Mary Danielli, and Geoffrey Parrinder, assisted by a large behind-the-scenes crew headed by Richard de la Mare, Ann and Geoffrey Faber, Alan Pringle, Peter du Sautoy, and the entire Book Committee at Faber and Faber, with T. S. Eliot, Dylan Thomas and other British literary luminaries putting in vital cameo appearances. Amos Tutuola remains the star of the show, but his performance never would have reached the limelight had it not been for the intelligence, devotion and courage of his supporting cast. One and all deserve our grateful applause.[54]

NOTES

1. The fullest accounts can be found in Harold Collins, *Amos Tutuola,* (New York: Twayne, 1969), pp. 17-25, and in my "Amos Tutuola: Debts and Assets," *Cahiers d'études africaines,* 10 (1970), 306-34, reprinted in *Critical Perspectives on Amos Tutuola,* ed. Bernth Lindfors (Washington, D.C.: Three Continents Press, 1975), pp. 275-306.

2. "A Life in the Bush of Ghosts," *West Africa,* 1 May 1954, pp. 389-90, reprinted in *Critical Perspectives on Amos Tutuola,* pp. 35-38. This is one of the best early sources of biographical data on Tutuola.

3. Tutuola places a definite article before the word "Ghosts" in the title of the story.

4. Letter from Amos Tutuola to Bernth Lindfors dated 11 September 1978.

5. From my tape-recorded interview with Tutuola in Ibadan on 18 July 1978.

6. Letter from A. Kraszna-Krausz to Bernth Lindfors dated 7 July 1978.

7. I am grateful to A. Kraszna-Krausz for this information. A fuller account of the tale itself appears in my "Amos Tutuola's Earliest Long Narrative," *Journal of Commonwealth Literature,* 16, 1, (August 1981), 45-55. This paper was originally prepared for presentation at the Ibadan Conference on the African Novel on 14 July 1978.

8. For a discussion of this kind of structure, see Gerald Moore, "Amos Tutuola: A Nigerian Visionary," *Black Orpheus,* 1 (1957), 27-35, reprinted in *Critical Perspectives on Amos Tutuola,* pp. 49-57.

9. "The Wild Hunter in the Bush of the Ghosts" ms., p. 44; *The Palm-Wine Drinkard and His Dead Palm-Wine Tapster in the Deads' Town* (London: Faber and Faber, 1952), pp. 31-8; Phebean Itayemi and P. Gurrey, *Folk Tales and Fables* (London: Penguin, 1953), pp. 46-50. Tutuola also uses this character in a short story, "Ajantala, the Noxious Guest," in *An African Treasury,* ed. Langston Hughes (New York: Crown, 1960), pp. 121-27, and a "forest burglar" by the same name can be found in his *The Brave African Huntress* (London: Faber and Faber, 1958), pp. 121-32. Ajantala also appears in D. O. Fagunwa's first novel, *The Forest of a Thousand Daemons,* trans. Wole Soyinka (London: Nelson, 1968), pp. 106-15.

10. (London: Nelson, 1938). The earliest edition of this book listed in Janheinz Jahn and Claus Peter Dressler's *Bibliography of Creative African Writing* (Nendeln, Liechtenstein: Kraus-Thomson, 1971), is the 1950 reprint, but A. Olubummo cites the first edition in "D. O. Fagunwa: A

Yoruba Novelist," *Odu, 9,* (September 1963), p. 26, as does Ayo Bamgbose, *The Novels of D. O. Fagunwa* (Benin City: Ethiope Publishing Corp., 1974), p. 131.

11. From my tape-recorded interview with Tutuola in Ibadan on 18 July 1978.

12. Arthur Calder-Marshall, review of *The Palm-Wine Drinkard* in *The Listener,* 13 November 1952, p. 819, reprinted in *Critical Perspectives on Amos Tutuola,* pp. 9-10.

13. *The Palm-Wine Drinkard,* pp. 40 and 53.

14. *West Africa,* 1 May 1954, p. 389, reprinted in *Critical Prespectives on Amos Tutuola,* p. 36. In a letter to me dated 11 June 1968, Tutuola revealed that he found the advertisement in *Nigeria Magazine.* This he confirmed in a tape recorded interview in Ibadan on 18 July 1978.

15. Letter from Mary Senior to Amos Tutuola dated 10 March 1950.

16. Letter from Mary Senior to Bernth Lindfors dated 1 July 1968.

17. Letter from Mary Senior to Amos Tutuola dated 23 October 1950.

18. Letter from Jocelyn Oliver to Bernth Lindfors dated 21 June 1968.

19. Letter from Mary Senior to Amos Tutuola dated 19 Februrary 1951.

20. Letter from Jocelyn Oliver to Bernth Lindfors dated 21 June 1968.

21. Letter from Jocelyn Oliver to Bernth Lindfors dated 14 July 1968.

22. Letter from Jocelyn Oliver to Richard de la Mare dated 19 February 1951.

23. Letter from Geoffrey Faber to Daryll Forde dated 15 March 1951.

24. Letter from Daryll Forde to Geoffrey Faber dated 19 March 1951.

25. Letter from Ann Faber to Jocelyn Oliver dated 31 May 1951.

26. Letter from Mary Senior to Ann Faber dated 1 June 1951.

27. Letter from Alan Pringle to Amos Tutuola dated 21 June 1951.

28. Letter from Amos Tutuola to Faber and Faber dated 27 June 1951.

29. Letter from Alan Pringle to Amos Tutuola dated 16 July 1951.

30. Letter from Amos Tutuola to Faber and Faber dated 20 July 1951.

31. Letter from Alan Pringle to Amos Tutuola dated 3 August 1951.

32. Letter from Amos Tutuola to Faber and Faber dated 27 August 1951.

33. Letter from Amos Tutuola to Faber and Faber dated 3 October 1951.

34. Letter from Alan Pringle to Amos Tutuola dated 11 October 1951.

35. Letter from Amos Tutuola to Faber and Faber dated 13 November 1951 and recopied in a letter from Tutuola to Faber and Faber dated 24 February 1952.

36. Letter from L. R. Simmons to Amos Tutuola dated 12 December 1951 and recopied in a letter from Tutuola to Faber and Faber dated 24 February 1952. Tutuola appears to have been the first author from Nigeria that Faber and Faber had published; this may account for the unfamiliarity of their business office with income tax agreements between Nigeria and Britain.

37. See, for example, Yemi Ogunbiyi, "Amos Tutuola in an Ocean of Sharks," *Daily Times* (Lagos), 10 June 1978, p. 21; Anon., "Cultural Plunder," *Daily Times* (Lagos), 15 June 1978, p. 3; and Kole Omotoso, "African Writers and Original Manuscripts, " *Afriscope*, 4, 1 (1974), 55, 57.

38. Letter from Amos Tutuola to Faber and Faber dated 21 March 1952.

39. Letter from Richard de la Mare to Jocelyn Oliver dated 13 July 1951.

40. Letter from Richard de la Mare to Jocelyn Oliver dated 19 July 1951.

41. Letter from Peter F. du Sautoy to Kurt Wolff dated 25 September 1951.

42. Letter from Kurt Wolff to Peter F. du Sautoy dated 7 January 1952.

43. Letter from Peter F. du Sautoy to Kurt Wolff dated 16 January 1952.

44. Letter from Kurt Wolff to Peter F. du Sautoy dated 18 March 1952.

45. Letter from Eric P. Swenson to Peter F. du Sautoy dated 25 June 1952.

46. Letter from Peter F. du Sautoy to Eric P. Swenson dated 4 July 1952.

47. See letter from Amos Tutuola to Faber and Faber dated 11 January 1952, and the reply from Alan Pringle to Tutuola dated 8 February 1952.

48. Tutuola was offered a contract for "My Life in the Bush of Ghosts" on 23 April 1953, in a letter from Alan Pringle.

49. See the letter from Mary Danielli to Alan Pringle dated 16 December 1952, and the letters from Geoffrey Parrinder to Alan Pringle dated 3 February 1952, and 27 March 1953.

50. *The Young Visiters, or, Mr. Salteena's Plan* (New York: Doran, 1919), written by Daisy Ashford, was introduced by J. M. Barrie as "the unaided effort in fiction of an authoress of nine years" (p. vii). Like *The Palm-Wine Drinkard*, it includes a photographic reproduction of one

page from the original, error-bestrewn manuscript. Perhaps it was Eliot's idea to include such a page in *The Palm-Wine Drinkard.*

51. Reader's report on "My Life in the Bush of Ghosts" dated Quinquagesima 1952 and signed "T. S. E." The last sentence of this typed report is hand-written, suggesting that it was either an afterthought or an attempt to soften an otherwise negative conclusion to the report. Curiously enough, the quotation singled out for praise by T. S. Eliot appears to have been deleted from the story when it was edited for publication by Geoffrey Parrinder.

52. According to a letter from Peter F. du Sautoy to George Braziller (dated 15 January 1953) which acknowledged receipt of Braziller's advance on royalties, this was done on 9 January 1953. Faber and Faber notified Tutuola of this transaction on the same day (see the letter from Peter F. du Sautoy to Tutuola dated 15 January 1953), informing him that his share of the advance (ninety percent, as agreed in the original contract) would reach him shortly. According to a letter from Peter F. du Sautoy to Barney Rosset dated 5 February 1962, the contract with Braziller is officially dated 12 February 1952; this may have been the date when all the necessary signatures had been acquired.

53. See the letters of Donald Allen of Grove Press to Peter F. du Sautoy dated 26 February 1953, 5 March 1953, 9 March 1953, 20 March 1953, and 8 April 1953. As noted earlier (in footnote 48) Faber and Faber offered Tutuola a contract for this book on 23 April 1953.

54. I must also extend my personal thanks to Amos Tutuola, A. Kraszna-Krausz, Mary Senior, Jocelyn Oliver, and to the staff of Faber and Faber for responding to numerous inquiries and for allowing me to quote verbatim from their letters. I am especially grateful for the courteous assistance I have received over the years from several individuals at Faber and Faber, particularly Sarah Lloyd, Rosemary Goad, Henry Mount Charles, Constance Cruikshank, Matthews Evans and Anthony Goff.

Author's Note:

A "Proper Farewell" to Amos Tutuola

One of Africa's most extraordinary literary pioneers passed away on 7 June 1997, and fellow Nigerians mourned his departure with reverential tributes and affectionate farewells. Authors, journalists and literary critics paid their respects to Amos Tutuola by praising the unique contribution he made to Nigerian literature by publishing nearly fifty years ago the nation's first full-length prose narrative in English, *The Palm-Wine Drinkard*. No fewer than five national dailies carried lengthy editorials summing up his career and achievements. To all of them he was a hero, a legend, a spellbinding raconteur—indeed, a storytelling genius. The *Sunday Tribune* called him a "literary colossus who took the world by storm" (Ukanah 4). The *Daily Champion* hailed him as "a literary icon...whose death has created a vacuum that will be difficult to fill" (Anon. 4). The *Weekend Concord* went further, claiming he was "Nigeria's Nobel Literature Laureate who never won" (Awoyinfa 6-7). The *Daily Times* asserted that Tutuola's "novels...set the stage early enough for the modern trend in literature of what has been described as magical realism," a term the editorial writer went on the define as "a fruitful combination of magic with realism" (Anon. 10). The *Post Express* credited him with a "remapping of the structural geography of the novel, by infusing an animistic effervescence and extravagance to the form, thereby clearing a path for the other African writers to follow" (Anon. 6). Tutuola was now an honored ancestor, an inspirational father figure to a whole generation of younger writers. Several journalists who had interviewed him in earlier years referred to him fondly as Pa Tutuola.

This posthumous praise-singing might have been music to Tutuola's ears had he been able to hear it, for at the outset of his career he had been subjected to abuse from Nigerian critics who felt embarrassed or annoyed by the kind of writing he did. His imperfect grasp of English, his obvious borrowings from Yoruba folktales, and his popularity in Europe and America as a naive primitivist alienated the educated elite who dismissed his work as childish and unsophisticated. Some even accused him of plagiarizing Daniel Fagunwa's more polished "phantasia novels" in Yoruba. It wasn't until the mid-1970s, when several prominent writers and critics (most notably Chinua Achebe) sought to reappraise his work, that Tutuola began to win a measure of respect at home. But in his later years he was virtually ignored by the indigenous literati, who perhaps viewed him as a cultural dinosaur, a throwback to an earlier era.

The posthumous praise-singers and obituary writers, well aware of this painful history of calumny and neglect, wanted to see something done to recuperate Tutuola's reputation. They felt he deserved a place of pride in the pantheon of Nigerian letters as well as some form of tangible recognition commensurate with his path-breaking accomplishments. Femi Osofisan was one of the first to offer a few concrete proposals:

> The only way we as a nation can begin to redeem ourselves is to give this man a proper farewell. And by this, I don't mean just the burial ceremony which I hope the nation will take seriously, but I am also talking of the even more important rites of remembrance by giving his works a greater prominence in our curriculum, enshrining his memory in some permanent symbol and so on (Balogun 2)...The house he lived in and worked [in] for example should become a national monument. It should become an important place to which children, tourists and visitors to our country should be taken to...Such people who have contributed so much to the cultural upliftment of our country ought to be placed on some kind of remuneration before their exit. That is how it is done in civilized societies. (Balogun 25)

A week later Cyprian Ekwensi weighed in with his own proposals, which the *Weekend Concord* highlighted with a back-page headline in one-inch type stating "ABACHA MUST HONOUR TUTUOLA." Ekwensi's argument was that

> Recognition in Nigeria today is based on how much money a man has...People want to know the cars he owns, the clothes he wears. Nobody asks how people get money. Nobody bothers about excellence in anything.
>
> Let Abacha do something for Tutuola, a man who excelled in his writing, a man who brought honour to Nigeria. It's a symbolic way of telling Nigerians that it is not only footballers and politicians that are recognised in this country. That the dogged pursuit of excellence in all fields of endeavour will be recognised and rewarded...
>
> It's unfortunate that we have no government-recognised or government-supported annual event for reward of those who excel in literature...Such a thing can be done and administered through the Nigerian Book Foundation. Government can name something or a place in the National Theatre or other relevant public place after him. A statue of him can be made and placed in a strategic culturally relevant area.
>
> We have places like halls in the universities named after politicians. What stops the same being done for writers? This is the way government can subtly change the values of people to appreciate excellence and doggedness. Government can also give a reasonable financial grant to his family or give scholarship to his children in school.

Ekwensi also recommended the establishment of an annual Amos Tutuola Prize for Literature. He went on to offer a very original appraisal of Tutuola's prose style:

> Tutuola wrote music with his words. Although his medium was prose, his writing appeared more musical, more lyrical and more poetic than many of those who actually set out to write poetry. His writing was in a class of its own, because he wrote out of a poetic mind though with grammatical limitations. Nigeria will never have

> another Tutuola. Were he to write today, he will never have written a book like *The Palm-Wine Drinkard. The Palm-Wine Drinkard* was [a] product of a phase in Nigerian literature that has passed. That phase can never come again and that is why *The Palm-Wine Drinkard* remains a classic—a book the type of which is not likely to be written again.

Ekwensi did not want Nigeria to wait until Tutuola was again honored abroad before the government acted.

> When *The Palm-Wine Drinkard* was first published in 1952 Nigerian critics booed it...They never recognised that he was creating a type of music with his writing. All their appreciation came only after the man was hailed abroad. (Sokunbi, 27, 32).

Many of the obituaries listed the honors Tutuola had received during his lifetime. These included such foreign awards as an honorary fellowship in the International Writing Program at the University of Iowa, a United States Information Agency (USIA) travel grant for participation in the International Visitors Program, and the prestigious Grimzane and Cavour prize in Italy. He had also been made an Honorary Fellow of the Modern Language Association of America (Chinua Achebe and Wole Soyinka being the only other Nigerians so honored) as well as an honorary citizen of New Orleans. In addition, the Pan-African Writers Association, an organization based in Ghana, had recognized his contribution to the African literary world by designating him a Noble Patron of the Arts.

But not all his kudos came from abroad. Nigerian organizations had honored him too. In 1979 he had been appointed a writer-in-residence at the University of Ife, in 1995 he had had the Meridian Award conferred on him by the Odu Themes Meridian theater group, and in 1996 he had received a Special Fellowship Award from the Oyo State Chapter of the National League of Veteran Journalists. Furthermore, two of his books had been adapted in Nigeria for the stage, the most famous of the them, *The Palm-Wine Drinkard*, having been produced as a

Yoruba opera by Kola Ogunmola as early as 1963 and again more recently by Chuck Mike's Collective Artistes Workshop. *My Life in the Bush of Ghosts* had been staged both by Demas Nwoko and Bode Sowande, the latter taking it to the United Kingdom as the Nigerian drama entry for the Africa '95 Festival held in London.

However, even these local and international successes did not quiet some of Tutuola's detractors. For instance, the National Association of Nigerian Theatre Arts Practicioners (NANTAP) had opposed the decision to take Sowande's production of *My Life in the Bush of Ghosts* to London on the grounds that it portrayed Nigerians as primitive people and did not truly represent contemporary African or Nigerian theater (Adebiyi 11). Nigeria's Minister of Information shared NANTAP's low opinion of the production, largely because he imagined it would convey a misleading and derogatory image of Africa to the outside world (Oribioye 15).

This complaint about Tutuola's work continued to be a theme in remarks made after Tutuola's death by two Nigerian lecturers in literature. B. M. Ibitokun of Obafemi Awolowo University was quoted as saying that

> approached from a nationalistic angle, which seeks to project the image of Nigeria to the outside world, Tutuola's genius is a freak, an ignominy both in terms of linguistic crudities and old-fashioned thematic preoccupations...[His works are] replete with linguistic ineptitudes from which even the most sympathetic reader will flinch (Akanni B4).

T. A. Oyesakin of Lagos State University raised the additional point that there was nothing new about Tutuola's stories, at least not to his indigenous audience.

> If you translate the works to Yoruba language a Yoruba man—who doesn't speak any other language—would simply assume that you are boring him with a story he listens to on a daily basis. By 15, a typical Yoruba child is conversant with the folktales. And in telling them, you bring in your own additive...[Tutuola] follows the

> traditional pattern of story telling, but he did not do so creatively. In other words, he did not put in the details which the African story teller would put in. He only makes do with the skeleton.

However, such stories might strike foreign readers as interesting and exotic, even while "confirming their conception of Africa as a dark continent" (Akanni B4). Tutuola, in other words, was still regarded as a dangerous barbarian by some of his countrymen. To this day his rehabilitation remains far from complete.

Yet it is clear that the process of reevaluation has begun and that Tutuola now has many more backers who insist his works, unusual as they are, merit inclusion in the Nigerian literary canon. A journalist and poet, Jare Ajayi, has spent the past ten years researching his life in order to write his biography. Oyekan Owomoyela, a Yoruba scholar based in the United States, is preparing a book-length critical study of his oeuvre. Tutuola may have died, but what he left to the world lives on.

For me, one of the most interesting features of the posthumous tributes was the amount of fresh biographical information they contained. For instance, although I had met and interviewed him several times, I did not know that he had four wives and eleven children. One journalist noted that Tutuola preferred to "keep his private life private" (Olabisi 16), and his eldest son Yinka confirmed this, stating that his father "would always keep mute on such matters" (Olabisi 16). However, Yinka added that Tutuola was a loving person not only to his peers but also to older and younger acquaintances:

> That too was radiating in the home and still radiates; he did not believe in partiality. He was fair to everybody and his wives knew what he wanted and he proved to be a good husband to them. So we did not experience the usual squabbles associated with polygamous households elsewhere. (Olabisi 16)

Tutola's eldest daughter, who refused to give her name to the press, said that she would miss him as a loving father, jokes cracker and counsellor. "He always advise[d] that one should be hardworking and should not be dependent." She also noted that some people from the neighborhood [came] to solicit her father's help in paying their school fees. (Ukanah 21).

Another daughter, Mrs. M. O. Oyewole, remembered him as "nice and generous" too, and his sister, Mrs. Fadeke Sobowale, reported that "he behaved to me as if he was the one that gave birth to me. My brother gave my son [a] standing fan and gave him N500 about 15 years ago" (Ukanah 21).

Tutuola's first wife believed that

> My husband would always be remembered for his genuine love for everyone and his transparent honesty...[In addition] my husband was a lover of nature and tradition. He was in love with animals and plants. Whenever he was on leave, he [left] the city for the village to study how animals behave. He was in harmony with the countryside...He was easily enticed to his culture which he struggled to preserve before his death. (Balogun 25).

A journalist said that in his later years Tutuola

> was surrounded often by his kith and kin from the neighbouring Abeokuta who look[ed] up to him for the settlement of occasional family squabbles and to preside over clan meetings...[He spent] the cool of the evenings attending prayer meetings at his home church, a branch of the Christ Apostolic Church (CAC) nearby. (Oribioye 15)

All these personal testimonies give us a fuller picture of Tutuola's character, especially his exceptional warmth, generosity and decency. He was a remarkable human being as well as a remarkable author.

Several reporters quoted from interviews with Tutuola that had appeared over the years in the Nigerian press, and Tutuola's own words help to convey a sense of how he regarded himself and his writing. He once explained that he began as an oral storyteller:

> [In school] we used to tell folktales to our school mates and teachers. Each time we got our holiday, I used to go to my people in the village. There was no radio or television but our source of amusement was to tell folktales after dinner. I used to listen to old people and the folktales they told. Each time I returned to school, I told the story to other school mates and I became a very good story teller. They used to give me presents for telling incredible folktales. (Adeniji 25)

However, when his father died, Tutuola's schooling was abruptly cut short and he had to go out and look for work. He eventually wound up as a messenger at the government Labour Department, and it was there and then that he conceived the idea of writing folktales down in the form of a connected narrative. His first effort, *The Wild Hunter in the Bush of the Ghosts*, which was modeled to some extent on D. O. Fagunwa's narratives in Yoruba, was submitted to a publisher of photography books in London, who wrote back to say that he could not publish it but wished to purchase the manuscript. With this fortuitous bit of encouragement, Tutuola went on to produce another lengthy narrative, *The Palm-Wine Drinkard and His Dead Palm-Wine Tapster in the Deads' Town* which, when published by Faber and Faber in 1952, launched Tutuola on his unlikely career as an internationally renowned author. Today this book is recognized as a significant milestone—indeed, the first milestone—in the long road that Nigerian authors writing in English have travelled since that time. It was equivalent to *The Canterbury Tales* in British literature, Tutuola being anglophone Africa's aboriginal Chaucer.

Throughout his career Tutuola saw himself as a folklorist dedicated to preserving Yoruba culture. He told interviewers

> I don't want the past to die. I don't want our culture to vanish. It's not good. We are losing [our customs and traditions] now but I'm still trying to being them into memory. (Awoyinfa 7)

His lack of higher education did not worry him or hold him back. He plunged on, writing as best he could in a language he had not completely mastered.

> So far as I don't want our culture to fade away I don't mind about English grammar. Even my publishers tell that I should write as I feel. I should feel free to write my story. I have not given my manuscript for anyone who knows grammar to edit. Only my publishers do everything relating to editing. (Awoyinfa 7)

Asked if he wasn't concerned that people abroad might laugh at him, he replied,

> Not at all. They know Nigerians are well-educated. They know Nigeria has so many educated people like Wole Soyinka, Chinua Achebe, Dr. Omotoso, Dr. Ogunbiyi and so forth. How could they because I am writing my own book be laughing at us and saying we don't know anything? Don't you see that is wrong? (Awoyinfa 7)

Besides, he realized that if he had had a better education, he might have become a worse writer.

> Probably if I had more education, that might change my writing or improve it or change it to another thing people would not admire. Well, I cannot say. Perhaps with higher education, I might not be as popular a writer. I might not write folktales. I might not take it as anything important. I would take it as superstition and not write in that line. (Awoyinfa 7)

However, he conceded that the type of writing he did might have hindered him from winning the respect of his countrymen. In an interview recorded in 1992 he said,

> Abroad people told me I am known [more] in other countries than in my own country. I know that I deserved honours for the past ten years. Because I don't boast. If you go through many magazines, they would say Amos Tutuola is the first man, the first African author to get international fame...perhaps the reason why Nigerian government does not give me any honour or so is because of my education. (Adebiyi 11)

It is encouraging to note that in the numerous obituaries in the Nigerian press, Amos Tutuola is finally being given due recognition for this achievements. The process of reassessing his contribution to the nation's verbal culture has begun in earnest, and it is unlikely that he will continue to be neglected by those concerned with codifying Nigeria's literary history. He was, after all, a hardy pioneer, one who survived and thrived, and as Gerald Moore remarked many years ago in one of the first serious essays on his work, he has grown much too large to ignore. The degree of reverence displayed in the posthumous tributes to him shows that his own journey to Deads' Town may yet yield the rewards and laurels denied him in his lifetime.

Fortunately, there is a shred of evidence to suggest that Tutuola may have been content with his lot in life. Writing itself may have provided him with adequate compensation of another sort. He once remarked that

> I feel happy when I am writing. When a writer starts writing, it is like seeing a picture or a vision. When the thing comes to the mind like this, you don't stop it until it vanishes away from the mind. And that time gives us happiness. (Awoyinfa 7).

Maybe it was this—the visionary experience of writing—that ultimately provided him with his greatest source of personal fulfilment.

Tributes to Amos Tutuola in the Nigerian Press

Adebiyi, Remi Edwards. "Passing of a Pioneer Novelist." *Guardian*, 14 June 1997, p. 11.

Adeniji, Olayiwola. "The Man and His Art." *Guardian*, 14 June 1997, p. 25.

Aiyetan, Dayo. "Amos Tutuola: Tribute to a Voyager." *Midweek Concord*, 18 June 1997, p. 22.

Akanni, Taofik. "Tutuola: Musings of a Story Teller." *Guardian on Sunday*, 15 June 1997, p. B4.

Anon. "Tutuola Dies at 77." *Nigerian Tribune*, 11 June 1997, p. 3.

___. "Amos Tutuola (1920-1997)." *Daily Times*, 14 June 1997, p. 10. (Editorial)

___. "Adieu, Amos Tutuola (1920-'97)." *Post Express*, 14 June 1997, p. 24.

___. "The Cases Tutuola Refused to Judge." *Nigerian Tribune*, 17 June 1997, p. 10.

___. "Amos Tutuola: Exit of a Literary Legend." *National Concord*, 20 June 1997, p. 9. (Editorial)

___. "The Legacy of Amos Tutuola (1920-1997)." *Post Express*, 21 June 1997, p. 6. (Editorial)

___. "Amos Tutuola." *Daily Champion*, 24 June 1997, p. 4. (Editorial)

___. "Adesina, Tutuola Bow Out." *African Concord*, 30 June 1997, p. 32.

___. "Amos Tutuola, 1920-1997." *Nigerian Tribune*, 1 July 1997, p. 7. (Editorial)

Arogbofa, 'Seinde. "Must Our Celebrities 'Die in Penury'?" *Daily Sketch*, 3 July 1997, p. 14; *Sunday Tribune*, 13 July 1997, p. 22.

Awoyinfa, Mike. "Amos Tutuola: Nigeria's Nobel Literature Laureate Who Never Won." *Weekend Concord*, 14 June 1997, pp. 6-7.

___. "Amos Tutuola's Nigeria." *Weekend Concord*, 21 June 1997, p. 2.

Balogun, Sola. "Tutuola, Novelist, Dies at 77." *Guardian*, 13 June 1997, pp. 1-2.

___. "Time Out for the Fabulist." *Guardian*, 14 June 1997, p. 25.

Biakolo, Tony. "'Pioneer' Tutuola's Exit." *Sunday Sketch*, 22 June 1997, p. 21; rpt. in *Sunday Vanguard*, 29 June 1997, p. 6.

Fadayiro, Koye. "Tutuola and His Palm-Wine." *Guardian*, 8 July 1997, p. 33.

Ibitokun, B. M. "Understanding Amos Tutuola." *Nigerian Tribune*, 24 June 1997, p. 15.

Ifowodo, Ogaga. "As Tutuola Goes to Deads' Town." *Post Express*, 5 July 1997, p. 24; 12 July 1997, p. 24.

Ighile, Osama, and Hameed Lawal. "The Silent Exit of a Literary Genius." *Daily Sketch*, 12 June 1997, p. 11.

Ipinmisho, Tunde. "There Goes the 'Ghost' Writer." *Daily Times*, 16 June 1997, p. 11.

Jimoh, Mike. "Tutuola, Writers, and the Media." *Post Express*, 21 June 1997, p. 24.

Okafor, Ndidi. "Tutuola's Place in Literary Development in Nigeria: Lecturers Speak." *Weekend Concord*, 21 June 1997, p. 2.

Olabisi, Kolawole. "Amos Tutuola's Unfulfilled Dreams." *Punch*, 18 June 1997, p. 16.

Oladunjoye, Rotimi. "Don't Soil My Good Name—Tutuola Tells Children Two Hours to His Death." *Tribune on Saturday*, 14 June 1997, p. 22.

Oribioye, Sunny. "Tutuola's Last Battle: Why Nigerian Govt Rejected His Story." *Daily Times*, 14 June 1997, p. 15.

Oshunkeye, Shola. "Poet Osundare Remembers Tutuola, an 'unignorable pioneer.'" *Weekend Concord*, 12 July 1997, p. 18.

Otiono, Nduka. "Tutuola's Family Seeks Financial Help for His Burial." *Post Express*, 21 June 1997, pp. 1-2.

Sokunbi, Wale. "Achaba Must Honour Tutuola—Ekwensi." *Weekend Concord*, 21 June 1997, pp. 27, 32.

Ukanah, Philip Oluwole. "The Last Wishes of Amos Tutuola—Son." *Sunday Tribune*, 15 June 1997, pp. 4, 21.

The Works of Janheinz Jahn

In *Through African Doors* Janheinz Jahn told of an amusing experience he once had when crossing the border between Dahomey and Nigeria. A Dahomean customs official, on seeing him describe himself on one of the customs forms as a writer, eagerly engaged him in conversation about Gide, Colette and several French West African poets and novelists he had read. Delighted to meet someone with whom he could discuss literature, the official offered to buy Jahn a beer and invited him to have a look at his library, but because Jahn was travelling in a car with others who were ready to depart, he could not accept these kind offers. A few miles further down the road at the Nigerian border station he had to fill out a similar form in order to reenter Nigeria. According to Jahn:

> The customs official watched intently every movement of the ball-point pen. In the little box for "profession" I put "writer," and in the one for "employed by" I put a stroke. I was going on to the next question when the official suddenly said: "Stop."
>
> "What is it?"
>
> "What is that you have written here" he asked. "There is no such profession. 'Writer' is a man who writes."
>
> "Exactly," I said, laughing.
>
> "Are you trying to make fun of me?" said the man, very conscious of the dignity of his office. "That is not a profession. Writing is something we all do. Anybody who can write could write 'writer' here. All Europeans are writers, but you are supposed to write your profession in this place."

> I tried to explain the thing to him. "'Writer' is not simply any man who writes. 'Writer' is a profession, it is the same as 'author.'"
>
> "Author?" The customs man had evidently not yet come across this word. The policeman, however, who had been casually listening to the conversation as he stamped the passport, now intervened. "'Author,'" he said, "I know that. I once read a book: *The Author of the Crime.* An author is the man who does it, a criminal." After this remark, philologically accurate enough, he gave me a piercing look and said: "What do you want in Nigeria, sir?"

Jahn tried to explain that he wrote books, and when this led to further confusion, he put it in the simplest terms he could:

> "I write something on paper, and what I write there is then printed."
>
> The customs man sighed with relief and gave a laugh of triumph. "Ah, now we have it, he is a journalist. But then, sir, you must fill in here what paper employs you."...
>
> "I am not employed by any paper; I write books."
>
> "Books are not written but printed," said the policeman.
>
> "So you are a printer," said the customs man. "Good, and now just tell us which firm of printers employ you."
>
> "But gentlemen," I protested, "I am not employed by any printers. Please try to understand: a 'writer' is free, as free as a poet."
>
> "I must warn you, sir," said the customs man, "you must not keep using words which are not proper words."
>
> I was starting to explain the word "poet" as well, when the policeman cut short the debate. "So you are an unemployed printer. That will do."[1]

And it was with this ignominious title that Jahn was permitted to cross the border.

This bizarre episode in cross-cultural misunderstanding was typical of Jahn's life. In some places in the world he received recognition for the work he did; in others—particularly in centers of learning where diplomas and certificates are regarded as passports to respectability—he was often eyed with suspicion because he earned his living by writing. There are still many customs officials performing duties in academic ivory towers who are unwilling to accept his credentials, who look upon him as no more than a journalist, a fast-talking author who committed his crimes in print. They claim that he misused words, that he frequently misled people by pretending to understand what no European could possibly fathom, that his translations of African culture were incorrect, that though he produced a lot of books he was never gainfully employed. Such policemen of the intellect might even now refuse to allow Jahn to enter another world with the word "scholar" beside his name.

Not that he would have coveted this title. Indeed, he might have considered it a mild insult. There were mindless academic tasks for which he had no appetite and certain kinds of scholarship for which he possessed neither patience nor respect. Jahn was not a pedant who concentrated on writing footnotes to other scholars' opinions. He was an original thinker with an audacious spirit, a pioneer willing to take risks with ideas, to speculate and hypothesize, to stir up controversy, to attack dogma. He believed in basing his theories on facts, but he was not afraid to allow his theoretical constructs to float free on the buoyancy of their own logic when it was impossible to adequately document everything he wanted to put forward. If he were asked to compose his own epitaph, he would probably still list himself simply as a writer rather than attempt to pass himself off as a scholar. Some might prefer that he be called a "creative writer" or "pseudo-scholar" because they find it difficult to persuade themselves to take the work of such a free-spirited individual seriously. But instead of merely calling Jahn names, let us review his career. To measure the achievements of any man, it is necessary to look back at his life and see what he did with it.

I know very little about Jahn's early life except what he told me in the spring of 1972 when he was living in my home while serving as Visiting Professor of English and of General and Comparative Studies at the University of Texas at Austin. After finishing dinner or a game of chess or several bottles of beer, we would sometimes sit and talk for hours, touching upon all kinds of subjects, including many of his past experiences. He was an entertaining conversationalist with a flair for drama and a talent for comic embroidery that often made me wonder how much of what he was telling me was really true. Now, several years later, I cannot vouch for the absolute accuracy of my own recollections either, but will try to reconstruct a few details about Jahn's life as faithfully as I can remember them. It should be understood, of course, that I do not claim to be speaking the whole truth and nothing but the truth about this unusual man.

Jahn was born in Frankfurt in 1918, the eldest of two sons in a wealthy family. When he was a young man, his parents had the means to send him to a different country each summer to learn a new language, and in this way he acquired a knowledge of four or five European tongues before entering the University of Munich where he studied, among other subjects, Classical Arabic. The Second World War interrupted his education, but his language ability earned him a noncombat position as an interpreter in the German Army. When the war ended, he did not go back to his studies but became a full-time writer. He took odd jobs as a journalist (including writing the horoscope columns for a daily newspaper), and his success in getting a few short stories published in literary magazines encouraged him to attempt writing a novel, which he later admitted was a complete failure. In the early 1950s he fell in love with a woman from a poor, working-class family with whom his bourgeois parents did not wish to be associated, much less related. When he ignored their protests and married her in 1955, his father disinherited him, leaving him penniless and completely on his own. These were lean, postwar years but Jahn's wife knew how to make ends meet on a skimpy budget, and they managed to survive on the little he earned as a free-lance writer.

The turning point in Jahn's life came in 1952 when Léopold Sédar Senghor, then a member of the French Parliament (and in 1960 to become President of Senegal), visited Frankfurt and gave a public lecture. Jahn was in the audience and, greatly stimulated by the ideas expressed, sought out Senghor afterwards to learn more about African literature and culture. By then Senghor had already published his first three volumes of poetry and only four years earlier had edited the remarkable *Anthologie de la nouvelle poésie nègre et malgache de langue française* with its famous introduction, "Orphée Noir," by Jean-Paul Sartre. Jahn was instantly seized with an ambition to translate these works into German, and he began to do research not only on the literature produced by Africans and West Indians in Paris but also on the cultural background from which it had sprung. He wanted to find out everything he could about African life styles, African social structure, African art, African symbolism, African thought. He read Lévy-Brühl, Frobenius and other early cultural anthropologists; he devoured a new French translation of Rev. Placide Tempels's *Bantu Philosophy* published in 1952 by Présence Africaine; he studied the works of Césaire, Damas and other originators of the Negritude movement. He also began perusing African-American literature, especially the works of poets and novelists associated with the Harlem Renaissance.

Soon he was writing about these authors, their books and their ideas. His first article on modern black poetry appeared in *Die Literatur* on August 15, 1952.[2] Within two years he was publishing essays on such varied topics as Bantu ontology and "The Contribution of the West Indians to Poetry," essays reflecting the range of his widening interests.

But his primary occupation during this period was translating into German the works of African, Afro-Caribbean and African-American writers. His first anthology, *Schwarzer Orpheus*, which borrows its title from Sartre's influential essay, appeared in 1954 and was an immediate success. A second edition was published the following year and a third in 1959; a new enlarged edition, brought out in 1964, was reissued in 1973 and is still in print today. It was the book that established Jahn's early reputation as a translator of the new black culture—not only the new expressive culture of Africa but also that of the African diaspora in the New World. A German scholar has attributed much of the success of *Schwarzer Orpheus* to its novelty: "Germans were surprised to discover that Africa had a literature apart from folktales, a written literature with new metaphors, rhythms and styles."[3] In his translations Jahn tried to remain faithful to these idioms, rendering Senghor's polyrhythmic lyricism, Césaire's surrealism, Langston Hughes's verbal jazz and blues into innovative Teutonic equivalents. In all, there were 82 poets represented in *Schwarzer Orpheus* by 161 poems; roughly one-third were African, one-third Caribbean and one-third African-American. Jahn's enthusiasm knew no geographical boundaries; he was interested in creative expression in the entire black world.

After the success of *Schwarzer Orpheus* he set to work to make the literatures of the black world better known in Germany. In 1955 he published *Tam-Tam Schwarz*, a book-length translation of Senghor's poetry, and the following year he published four books, including the first German translations of Césaire's poetry, of Césaire's first play, of Barbadian writer George Lamming's autobiographical novel *In the Castle of My Skin*, and of the poetry of Sam Allen, an African-American who wrote under the pseudonym "Paul Vesey." During this very fruitful period in the mid-1950s he also gave a number of radio talks on black literature, focusing sometimes on individual writers and sometimes on broader topics such as rumba rhythms in Afro-Cuban poetry, the language of modern African literature, or the black renaissance in Africa and the New World—topics which gave him the latitude to comment on new trends and timely issues in contemporary black culture. It may have been during one of these radio talks broadcast in 1957 that he first coined the term "Neo-African literature"[4] to distinguish the new writing emerging in the black world from the traditional oral literature which many Europeans still presumed to be the only mode of literary expression utilized by black peoples. Jahn was soon the major European publicist of black literary achievements the world over.

In September 1956 Jahn attended the first World Congress of Black Writers and Artists, which was convened in Paris by

Présence Africaine. There he met not only such illustrious authors as Richard Wright, George Lamming, Frantz Fanon, Jacques Rabemananjara, Ferdinand Oyono, Bernard Dadié, Davidson Nicol and Mercer Cook but also a German writer named Ulli Beier who had been teaching phonetics in Nigeria for several years and doing research on Yoruba culture. Jahn and Beier agreed that it would be an opportune moment to start a literary journal in Nigeria, one which would carry original works written in English by African and African-American authors and also English translations of poetry and prose by prominent writers from French and Portuguese areas of Africa and the New World. They decided to call the journal *Black Orpheus*, giving it the same title as Sartre's essay and Jahn's anthology.[5] The first issue appeared in September 1957 and within a few years *Black Orpheus* had established itself as the most influential literary journal in all of Africa. Beier, who continued to edit the magazine until the eruption of the Nigerian civil war in 1967, must of course be given most of the credit for *Black Orpheus*'s remarkable success. Jahn served as coeditor for only two years before being replaced by Ezekiel Mphahlele and Wole Soyinka. But Jahn was instrumental in getting this crucial literary venture started and he supported it with frequent contributions of critical essays even after he was no longer on the editorial board. *Black Orpheus* was another one of his pioneering efforts which led to greater international awareness and appreciation of modern black literatures.

Greater achievements were yet to come. By 1958 Jahn was already fairly well-known in Germany for his translations. In the six years since first meeting Senghor he had published twelve books, seven of them translations of novels, plays or collections of poetry by individual African, Afro-Caribbean and African-American authors, five of them anthologies of translated prose and poetry from the same areas as well as from Indonesia and the Hispano-Arabic world. He had also written nearly two dozen essays and given a score of radio talks during these active years. However, the book which was to earn him an international reputation, good and bad, was *Muntu: An Outline of Neo-African Culture*, published in 1958. By 1961 it was available in Swedish, English, American, French and Italian editions, and subsequently was translated into at least three more languages—Spanish, Norwegian and Dutch. *Muntu* was the book which transformed Jahn from a translator to an interpreter of modern black culture.

But Jahn's interpretation was controversial. Few reviewers took a neutral position on *Muntu*. Some praised it, some condemned it, some tempered praise for its analytical clarity with condemnation of its tendency toward sweeping generalizations and overstatements, some were impressed with Jahn's erudition, some were indignant about his lack of knowledge of many areas of Africa. The South African novelist Peter Abrahams, reviewing the book in the *New York Times Book Review*, called it

> a brilliant and painstaking piece of scholarship ... I think this is the first time that any Western writer has gone below the surface of what is glibly called "the African personality" and come up with a true picture. This, I think, is as near as anybody who is not himself an African will get to understanding what makes the African tick. This is how the African sees his world; these are his beliefs; and here, too, I think, the thoughtful reader will find an indication of what is likely to happen in tomorrow's continent.[6]

For Abrahams, Jahn was both a scholar and a seer. But for the anonymous reviewer in the London *Times Literary Supplement* Jahn was merely refurbishing old academic clichés and trying to give them a new respectability by clothing them in African terminology. His work was neither original nor African in its intellectual orientation.

> What Mr. Jahn has to say here about the significance of sacrifice, of ancestors, of spirit-cults and spirit possession, and of religious syncretism, has been a commonplace of ethnological studies for many years. But then so has almost everything African he refers to.

> If, as is claimed, this book is intended for the general public rather than for anthropologists or art-historians, so much the more important that it should embody a sense of proportion both about Africa and about what its readers might take for granted. The intelligence of the general public is certainly not overestimated here ... the use of a few African words does not save this modern view of Africa from being yet another reflection of European values, and such internal standards of criticism as an African culture might be supposed to have and to develop systematically never appear.[7]

Another British reviewer, Neal Acherson, writing in *The Spectator*, was even more scathing in his appraisal of *Muntu*:

> Mr. Jahn's essay on the elements of "the African culture" is strident with jargon and with existentialist arrogance ... His book has been cooked out of enormous reading with no discernible care or humility, and the bibliography is as menacing as a machine-gun belt. Essentially, on the other hand, it is not a work of scholarship at all. Assembling a number of classifying words from several African languages, Mr. Jahn then proclaims them master-concepts and selects whatever evidence he can find to fit them.

But the same reviewer then went on to say:

> And yet he scores. His philosophical apparatus of Modalities and Designations and Determinations does help to describe the nature of African creativity and shows it functioning both in Leadbelly in Texas and in the guitarist Jean-Bosco Mwenda in Katanga. No "African philosophy" exists in the usual sense, but the material for one is ready.[8]

In other words, *Muntu* was full of mystical popularized pseudo-science but somehow it worked. Despite his limitations and quirks, Jahn had managed to perform an impressive feat of intellectual voodoo in outlining neo-African culture.

It is not difficult to see why some Africanists were upset with *Muntu*. The book was ambitious in scope and polemical in tone. Since sub-Saharan Africa is huge and its people diverse in language, custom and belief, any attempt to "determine what is 'really African'" and then define "to what extent [African poetry, literature and art] are 'really African' and to what extent they are not"[9] would seem doomed to failure. It would be too easy for ethnologists, folklorists and literary critics familiar with Africa's complexity to cite counter-examples or to demonstrate where Jahn's theory did not fit the facts in a particular corner of Africa. Professional nit-pickers could have their fun poking holes in such an all-embracing hypothesis. And many did. Several were especially scornful of Jahn's nomenclature, pointing out that it was foolish to apply Bantu and Dogon philosophical terminology borrowed from Abbé Alexis Kagame, Placide Tempels and Marcel Griaule—words such as Muntu, Kintu, Hantu, Kuntu and Nommo—to non-Bantu and non-Dogon conceptual systems. What might be true for the Dogon of Mali or the Bantu peoples of Ruanda might not be equally true for the Tiv of Nigeria, the Luo of Kenya or the Khoisan peoples of Southern Africa. There were too many exceptions to consider for the theory to have uniform applicability to the entire continent, much less to the black diaspora.

Yet, as one disgruntled reviewer admitted, the system Jahn devised—artificial, schematic and simplistic as it was—did seem to work. It was a useful shorthand for expressing essential African ideas, a workable tool for probing certain African realities. Jahn may have ignored or overlooked numerous specific truths about Africa in order to make his total argument more coherent and persuasive, but in so doing he may have arrived at a much larger, more profound truth about at least one aspect of contemporary African experience—the persistence of tradition in modern black expressive culture. His contribution here was unique and unprecedented. He had attempted a synthesis and distillation of notions about the African arts such as no one had dared to attempt before. Whether he actually succeeded may still be open to debate but at least he tried to go beyond the usual boundaries of inquiry by plunging into uncharted territory. He was still functioning as a pioneer.

If *Muntu* had been published in 1975 instead of 1958, it probably would not have commanded so much attention. In the late 1950s and early 1960s the world was hungry for information about Africa because the colonial era was finally ending and new African nations were gaining their indepedence at a rate of one or two per month. Sociopolitical changes in Africa dominated the international news. *Muntu*, arriving at this time, provided a reasonably concise explanation of Africa's ability to adapt to cultural change without losing its identity. Such a book helped Europe and America to understand some of the forces at work in modern African society. *Muntu* was the thinking man's Baedeker to metamorphosis in the African continent.

After *Muntu*, Jahn began his bibliographical researches into black literature, publishing in 1959 (with John Ramsaran) a booklet entitled *Approaches to African Literature*, the first attempt at a bibliography of African writings. He also travelled through parts of West Africa in 1958-59, documenting his trip in *Through African Doors*, published in 1960. And of course he continued writing essays on African, Afro-Caribbean and African-American literatures.

Through African Doors is an amusing account of Jahn's adventures in Nigeria, Dahomey and Ghana. Eager for an authentic African experience, he eschewed European modes of transportation and travelled about on foot or bicycle or aboard African lorries, taxies, boats and trains, buying a third-class ticket whenever possible. He tried to acquire a taste for African food and a mastery of African table manners and other forms of indigenous etiquette. He fraternized with the high and the low, entering with equal curiosity the palaces of kings, the homes of the *nouveaux riche*, the sleazy nightclubs in the city and the rough huts of peasants in the country. Ever the enthusiastic student of African folkways, he sought in his daily experiences evidence to verify his theories of cultural change.

But he was not obsequious among his hosts. Sometimes he would deliberately provoke an argument when he found middle-class Africans attempting to emulate European ways. On other occasions he would put up with personal discomfort rather than allow his host to offer him accommodations superior to those an African visitor would be offered. Jahn did not want to be mistaken for a tender-skinned colonialist. As in his literary research, he jumped into new experiences with gusto, seeking to taste the full flavor of everything he came across. His appetite for adventure was insatiable.

Jahn spent the next few years involved in his usual academic activities. He translated more of Césaire and Senghor as well as a lengthy autobiographical novel by Bloke Modisane entitled *Blame Me On History*. He wrote more essays for journals, magazines and newspapers. He gave more talks on the radio, sometimes branching out into subjects such as African art and African medicine in addition to covering literary developments in the black world. In 1964 he made his first lecture tour of the United States. But his two major works during this phase of his career were *A Bibliography of Neo-African Literature from Africa, America and the Caribbean* (1965) and *A History of Neo-African Literature: Writing in Two Continents* (1966—German edition).

The *Bibliography* was another ground-breaking achievement. Although several specialized bibliographies on black literature had already appeared, none was as detailed or as comprehensive as Jahn's, which attempted to "list all the works which might be considered as belonging to neo-African literature."[10] This took in not only writings by Africans but also writings by Afro-Caribbeans and African-Americans. Moreover, if Jahn's stylistic criteria for the identification of neo-African literature were followed rigorously, even the works of Euro-African and Euro-American writers could be included if they manifested "the overlapping of two historically different literatures: 1) traditional Negro-African literature, and 2) Western literature."[11] However, Jahn admitted that such stylistic discriminations were difficult to make and subject to dispute, so until his criteria could be further refined and applied with some analytical precision, he was content to list all creative works—essays and unpublished manuscripts as well as novels, plays, volumes of poetry, and autobiographies—produced by black writers in Africa and the New World. In other words, his bibliography included rather than excluded writings that failed to meet his own "neo-African" criteria. This must be stressed because several obtuse reviewers unjustly accused him of deliberately omitting a number of black authors because their writings did not manifest what Jahn was imagined to regard arbitrarily as the hallmarks of "neo-African style." As Jahn said clearly in his introduction,

> Whether the user agrees or disagrees with my definition of neo-African literature, whether he interprets my term 'neo-African literature' as meaning 'modern literature in Negro-Africa,' 'literature of Negro-Africans and Afro-Americans' or 'Negro literature,' he will find the related works in this volume.[12]

Following this catholic principle, Jahn was able to list 3566 works by more than 1400 authors, recording each volume in the fullest possible bibliographical detail. Literary anthologies and translations in thirty-eight different languages were included, too. Jahn's *Bibliography* immediately became the indispensable reference tool for any scholar working in black literatures. Indeed, it helped to establish such literatures as legitimate subjects for academic inquiry. Jahn, more than any other individual researcher, must be given credit for accelerating the pace of scholarly activity in these new literary fields.

But Jahn didn't confine himself to bibliographical endeavors. His book, *A History of Neo-African Literature: Writing in Two Continents*, published a year after the *Bibliography*, was one of the first scholarly works to attempt to cover the history of black writing in two worlds. Other scholars such as Bakary Traoré, Lilyan Lagneau-Kesteloot, Thomas Melone, Ezekiel Mphahlele, Gerald Moore, Judith Gleason and Claude Wauthier had examined more restricted topics in some detail, but no one had tried systematically to relate the literature of Africa to those of black America and the Caribbean.

Any effort to do this was bound to be controversial, and Jahn's *History* got the same mixed reaction from critics and reviewers as *Muntu* had received eight years earlier. Readers were impressed with Jahn's wide-ranging research which took him into such remarkably varied areas as sixteenth-century Latin poetry by Alfonso Alvares (the first known Negro writer), African praise-songs, Hausa and Swahili traditions of verse, early Southern Bantu writings, African-American slave narratives, New World minstrelsy and voodoo, Negro spirituals, blues and calypso, the Harlem Renaissance, Cuban Negrism and the evolution of Negritude. But while critics were willing to concede that Jahn had done an enormous amount of reading and thinking on these heterogeneous subjects, they were still suspicious of his underlying theory and felt that some of his ideas, though extremely stimulating, were not adequately proven by the few examples he cited or the brief analyses he offered. They were also upset once again by his terminology, especially by the new word he coined for sub-Saharan Africa—Agisymba. The reaction of the reviewer in the *Times Literary Supplement* to the original German edition of Jahn's *History* was typical of the bemused skepticism that greeted this ambitious book:

> His theory seems to be that the black African cultures south of the Sahara form a cultural unit. In spite of local differences they share basic, philosophic concepts. Herr Jahn assumes that he has proved this in his earlier book *Muntu*. In this new volume he takes it for granted that readers have accepted his argument that Alexis Kagame's controversial book *Bantu Philosophy* is valid, by and large, for the whole of Negro Africa and he can therefore proceed to give this country a name: Agisymba is what we are expected to call this territory now. Herr Jahn found the word on an old map of Africa drawn by Ptolemy. There it seemed to signify all those countries which Ptolemy knew nothing about. It would be kinder not to draw the comparison.

But even after this negative opening and a few examples of Jahn's inability to demonstrate some of his theories, the anonymous *Times* reviewer felt compelled to add that Jahn's *History* had some redeeming qualities:

> Herr Jahn's new book is full of such bold ideas, most of them unproved, but many worth discussing. Like *Muntu* and other writings by this prolific apostle of negritude, *Geschichte der neoafrikanischen Literatur* leaves the reader entirely unconvinced but greatly stimulated and entertained.[13]

This, it could be argued, was Jahn's primary achievement as a scholar. He was able to provoke, to stimulate and to entertain. He didn't seek definitive proof of many of his ideas because often there was not enough evidence available to examine. His role was that of an instigator, someone who goaded others into activity by suggesting something they could test independently by examining a larger body of evidence. As Jahn himself stated in the first chapter of his *History*:

> When considering a living literature like the neo-African, historians of literature must expect to be deepening and widening their observations all the time. An introduction to the neo-African literature, in fact, is neither a complete history of this literature nor a conclusive study of its styles; a great deal of further research is needed before works of that sort can be carried out. The purpose of the present book is to point out the problems and classify provisionally the material to be analysed.[14]

In other words, Jahn was not attempting to provide unassailable answers to the riddles posed by this new literature; he was merely trying to raise relevant questions which others could investigate in greater depth and detail. He was urging scholars and academicians to explore thoroughly new frontiers. And when he himself sought to make bold leaps forward into these unknown regions, he was still being stopped at the border by literal-minded customs officials who suspected his papers were not in order.

After writing his *History*, Jahn returned to his habitual activities, producing two or three major translations and anthologies each year in addition to publishing essays, broadcasting radio talks and lecturing on African literature at the University of Frankfurt. Between 1966 and 1970 he translated books by Senghor, Césaire, V.S. Naipaul, Roger Mais, Cameron Duodu and Marcel Griaule as well as all the material which went into three anthologies of African, West Indian and African-American tales, proverbs, songs and love stories. He wrote and spoke on Negritude, on Senghor, on the cultural festivals he attended in Dakar, Algiers and Ife, on academic conferences and book fairs, on the growth and development of African literatures, on corruption, magic and polygamy in modern Africa—on literally anything that interested him. He also edited for Kraus-Thomson Reprints a critical selection of the earliest and most important African and West Indian literary works, journals and scholarly monographs. He was now internationally recognized as a leading authority on African and New World black culture, and his talents were in great demand.

His next major opus was the comprehensive *Bibliography of Creative African Writing* which he compiled with the assistance of Claus Peter Dressler, a trained librarian who had worked for him for several years and had helped to collect, transcribe and record data for his earlier *Bibliography of Neo-African Literature*. The new bibliography was even more impressive than the first, though it was far narrower in scope, covering only the creative writing produced in sub-Saharan Africa. Jahn and Dressler managed to list 2130 individual works by 1127 authors writing in 51 African languages as well as in English, French and Portuguese. They also provided full documentation on 202 anthologies, 36 literary magazines, 33 bibliographies and 8 "forgeries" or works published by non-Africans under African pseudonyms. But the greatest improvement in coverage lay in the inclusion of bibliographical data on the hundreds of books and essays that had been written on African literatures; this important body of critical and scholarly commentary had never been adequately recorded in one volume before, and though Jahn and Dressler's coverage was by no means complete, their new *Bibliography* provided the most comprehensive single source of information yet compiled on the vast and widely scattered secondary literature that had grown up so rapidly around several of the new literatures of sub-Saharan Africa. In addition, their coverage of the primary works was remarkably thorough, embracing not only the various editions in which each title had appeared but also all known translations in 45 different languages of the world. This book instantly became the bibliographical Bible for all denominations of scholars working in African literatures. If Jahn had done nothing else in his lifetime, this *Bibliography* alone would have earned him an international reputation as a scholar.

But of course he did much more than this. His next book was another fundamental reference work, *Who's Who in African Literature: Biographies, Works, Commentaries,* which he completed in 1972 in collaboration with two of his closest associates, Ulla Schild and Almut Nordmann. Again, nothing quite like it had ever been done for African literature before. The book contained basic biographical information on nearly 450 African authors as well as a selection of diverse critical opinions on their works taken from standard secondary sources. Whenever possible, Jahn and his co-editors made an effort to contact the authors personally or by mail to check on the biographical data they had collected; they had also scoured maps of Africa trying to verify the existence of all the towns, districts and geographical features mentioned in their research notes on individual writers. The result, they admitted, was "not wholly balanced" since some of the information they sought could not be obtained, but it was nonetheless the fullest biographical handbook that had been produced on the lives of African writers. As such, it was an indispensable companion to Jahn and Dressler's *Bibliography,* to which it had been keyed by numerous cross-references to avoid unnecessary repetition of basic bibliographical data. Jahn, with the help of his collaborators, had scored another impressive first in African literary studies.

It was to be his last major contribution. Within a year he was dead, having suffered several heart attacks after recovering from a long illness contracted while leading a group of wealthy tourists through West Africa to the land of the Dogon. He died at home on October 20, 1973, just two days after interviewing for German television the African poet who had launched him on his career twenty-one years earlier—Léopold Sédar Senghor. It was a fitting conclusion to a life dedicated to disseminating information about literary and cultural achievements in modern Africa.

Throughout his career Jahn remained a tireless worker who never lost his enthusiasm for his chosen vocation. He thrived on accepting challenges which tested his mental and physical resources, making demands on his enormous fund of creative energy. Though he had an eye for detail and meticulous accuracy, he never stooped to trivial or petty pursuits which would not advance understanding and appreciation of black expressive cultures. Through his translations, anthologies, bibliographies, interpretations, lectures, essays and numerous controversies, he contributed more than anyone else to world-wide recognition of Africa's unique contributions to twentieth-century civilization. He was Africa's best literary agent and promoter.

How did he succeed in accomplishing all he did? How did he manage to find the time and stamina to write, translate, edit and compile fifty-four books in the last two decades of his life? How did he keep up such a hectic pace year after year and still maintain the ability to travel, lecture and enjoy life as much as he did? His secret, he once told me with a twinkle in his eye, was that he didn't really write his books; he dictated them. A tape recorder was his amanuensis. Even *Muntu*, he insisted, had been put together from the transcripts of a series of lectures he had delivered orally. Translations were even easier. He merely read a work, circling the words he did not know, then asking his friends and assistants to look these up in a dictionary and to write their German equivalents in the margins. After this had been done, he would sit down with the book again and read his translation of it onto cassette tapes, which unemployed housewives in his village would transcribe to earn a little pocket money. In this way he was able to translate very speedily lengthy books or the numerous excerpts included in his anthologies. It took a bit longer to assemble a scholarly book using such methods but he claimed this was how he usually first got his ideas down on paper. Later he would revise and polish up the transcript but his work at that stage would be mainly editorial. When formulating his ideas or translating a text, he always relied more heavily on his tongue than on his pen.

Though Jahn may have been exaggerating slightly for dramatic effect (it is inconceivable, for example, that his newspaper articles could have been composed in this manner), his account of his methods of composition nevertheless sheds interesting light on his working habits and personality. In his own writings he fused oral and written modes of communication, shaping his African material into recognized and accepted forms of European expression. Thus, in a sense, he himself was operating according to neo-African artistic principles. He had bridged not just two disparate cultures but two disparate techniques of creative expression. He was Germany's most African writer.

In an essay completed a few months before his death, Jahn appraised the career of Germany's most famous Africanist, Leo Frobenius. It was the Frobenius centennial year, and Jahn, with characteristic iconoclasm and calculated mischief, attacked the great man's scholarship and unscientific practices, debunking the theories and intuitions upon which his reputation was based. Instead of humbly placing a wreath on his tomb, Jahn defaced it with bold graffiti, labeling him a "demonic child," "a pacesetter of fascism," "a post-Wilhelminian barroom philosopher," "a retarded petty bourgeois," "a pseudo-scholar," "a sentimental author of *Kitsch*."[15] Yet Jahn also respected Frobenius for his enormous productivity, his huge collections of well-organized data, his vitality and his love for Africa. And he praised him for having made the world aware of the dignity and beauty of African art, literature and culture. "Africa," he said, "will remember him for that. He helped Africans and Afro-Americans to find a new consciousness of themselves within the African heritage."[16]

The same could be said of Jahn himself. Though his theories remain controversial, though some may still regard him as having been too enthusiastic and unscholarly in his approach to black expressive culture, though some might yet be tempted to call him the same names he called Frobenius, we cannot fail to be impressed with the monumental works he left behind. Nor can we deny him the credit he merits for having helped to make the world conscious of the cultural wealth of modern Africa. Janheinz Jahn deserves to be issued with a new international passport, one in which he is properly identified not as an unemployed printer but as a very important writer, certainly the most important writer on African literatures that Germany has yet produced.

NOTES

1. Janheinz Jahn, *Through African Doors* (London: Faber and Faber, 1962), pp. 141-42.

2. For a complete list of Jahn's writings, see Ulla Schild, "A Bibliography of the Works of Janheinz Jahn," *Research in African Literatures*, 5 (1974), 196-205.

3. Ulla Schild, "Janheinz Jahn, 1918-1973," *Research in African Literatures*, 5 (1974), 194.

4. In 1957 he gave a talk on "Zwischen zwei Zivilisationen: Eine Analyse der neoafrikanischen Literatur" on Hessischer Rundfunk. See Schild, "Bibliography," p. 204.

5. For a history of this journal, see my "A Decade of *Black Orpheus*," *Books Abroad*, 42 (1968), 509-16.

6. Peter Abrahams, "Africa on the Move," *New York Times Book Review*, 14 May 1961, p. 10.

7. *Times Literary Supplement*, 11 August 1961, p. 498.

8. *The Spectator*, 31 March 1961, pp. 451-52.

9. Janheinz Jahn, *Muntu* (New York: Grove Press, 1961), p. 21.

10. Janheinz Jahn, *A Bibliography of Neo-African Literature from Africa, America and the Caribbean* (London: Deutsch, 1965), p. viii.

11. Ibid., p. vii.

12. Ibid., p. viii.

13. *Times Literary Supplement*, 8 September 1966, p. 816.

14. Janheinz Jahn, *A History of Neo-African Literature: Writing in Two Continents* (London: Faber and Faber, 1966), pp. 23-24.

15. Janheinz Jahn, *Leo Frobenius: The Demonic Child* (Austin: African and Afro-American Studies and Research Center, University of Texas, 1974), pp. 17, 20.

16. Ibid., p. 20.

Courting the Hottentot Venus

On Thursday, September 20, 1810, an unusual advertisement appeared in London's *Morning Post*:

> THE HOTTENTOT VENUS.——— Just arrived (and may be seen between the hours of One and Five o'clock in the evening, at No. 225, Piccadilly), from the Banks of the River Gamtoos, on the Borders of Kaffraria, in the interior of South Africa, a most correct and perfect Specimen of that race of people. From this extraordinary phenomena [sic] of nature, the Public will have an opportunity of judging how far she exceeds any description given by historians of that tribe of the human species. She is habited in the dress of her country, with all the rude ornaments usually worn by those people. She has been seen by the principal Literati in this Metropolis, who were all greatly astonished, as well as highly gratified, with the sight of so wonderful a specimen of the human race. She has been brought to this country at a considerable expence, by Kendrick Cerar [sic], and their stay will be but of short duration.—To commence on Monday next, the 24th inst.——Admittance, 2s. each.

This cleverly worded announcement, implying prior endorsement by luminaries in polite society, was calculated to arouse public interest in the exhibition of a woman from one of the remotest reaches of the British Empire. The reference to "a most correct and perfect Specimen" who "exceeds any description given by historians of that tribe of the human species" suggested that this was a female remarkably well-formed and good-looking, a rare beauty capable of charming all who gazed upon her. The title she bore—"The Hottentot Venus"—

contributed more than a pinch of piquancy to an image of exotic, voluptuous allure.

But to anyone of that day who had heard anything at all about Hottentots and could read between the lines, the joke would have been obvious. Venus indeed! If this woman was typical of her people, she would not be a beauty queen by English standards but rather a monstrosity, an aberration of nature, a grotesque freak. Her most remarkable features would be a huge, steatopygous bottom and an elongated genital "apron," characteristics that were thought to link her more closely to baboons and monkeys than to human beings. Any "correct and perfect" specimen of Hottentot womanhood would have to exceed particular European anatomical norms to such an extent as to appear grossly misshapen, oddly malformed. Her perfection could only be spectacular imperfection, her voluptuousness a farce.

The coarse joke drew crowds. The show was not widely advertised in the weeks that followed so it may have owed its initial success to word-of-mouth endorsements from customers who had paid their two shillings to see this novel creature, but when a controversy arose in the press about the decency of her display—a dispute that ultimately had to be resolved in court—her notoriety grew until she became a household word. Songs, quips, spoofs and caricatures inspired by the "Hottentot Venus" began to circulate widely, transforming her into a phenomenon of the popular culture of her day.

She remained on the London stage for more than eight months, then toured the provinces for a while, and later resurfaced for a sixteen-month run in Paris, where she made a lasting impact not only on popular culture but also on natural science. After her premature death in 1815 she was dissected by Baron Georges Cuvier, the leading naturalist in France, who published a definitive report on her anatomical peculiarities. Other scientists followed Cuvier's lead, using this rare specimen as a basis for sweeping generalizations about the physical and cultural characteristics of certain native peoples of South Africa.

As a consequence, one bottom-heavy woman continued to influence the way Africans were perceived in Europe until ultimately she became reified as a biological concept, a scientifically sanctified racial cliché. Her skeleton, decanted brain and other remains are still preserved and studied at the Museé de l'Homme, where a plaster cast of her body, naked and unadorned, stood on public display until 1982. Thus, of all early nineteenth-century stage performers, the Hottentot Venus must he recognized as the one who has had the greatest overall exposure and the longest consecutive run.

But it is not her career in show business or science that interests us here. Rather, it is her day in court that prompts a fresh postmortem examination, for the controversy surrounding her exhibition and the manner in which her working conditions were investigated and her interests protected shed light on humanitarian impulses and legal constraints in the Romantic age. Let us see what kind of justice a Hottentot could expect in Georgian England.

First, the background to her case.[1] Sartjee Baartman (for that was her real name) had been conveyed to England by Hendric Cezar, a Boer farmer at the Cape who had formed a show business partnership with Alexander Dunlop, a British army surgeon on an African ship. Dunlop, accompanying Cezar and Sartjee to London, had tried to sell his share in her, as well as a giraffe skin, to William Bullock, a prosperous antiquarian who owned a museum of art and natural history. Bullock had bought the skin but refused the Hottentot, so Dunlop had sold out to his partner Cezar, who began exhibiting her in London with such success that Dunlop soon regretted having so rashly relinquished his interest in her. Sartjee apparently had taken no part in these negotiations, even though she may have been the one most affected by the outcome.

The show itself was described in a report in the *Times* as taking place on

> a stage raised about three feet from the floor, with a cage, or enclosed place at the end of it; that the Hottentot was within the cage; that on being ordered by her keeper, she came out, and that her appearance was highly offensive to delicacy...The Hottentot was produced like a wild beast, and ordered to move backwards and forwards, and come out and go into her cage, more like a bear in a chain than a human being...She frequently heaved deep sighs; seemed anxious and uneasy; grew sullen, when she was ordered to play on some rude instrument of music...And one time, when she refused for a moment to come out of her cage, the keeper let down the curtain, went behind, and was seen to hold up his hand to her in a menacing posture; she then came forward at his call, and was perfectly obedient...She is dressed in a color as nearly resembling her skin as possible. The dress is contrived to exhibit the entire frame of her body, and the spectators are even invited to examine the peculiarities of her form.[2]

Some of the spectators accepted this invitation by touching her rump and searching for evidence of padding or some other artifice beneath her skimpy, skin-colored dress. A woman who saw the show reported that

> One pinched her, another walked round her; one gentleman *poked* her with his cane; and one *lady* employed her parasol to ascertain that all was, as she called it, "*nattral.*" This inhuman baiting the poor creature bore with sullen indifference, except upon some great provocation, when she seemed inclined to resent brutality, which even a Hottentot can understand. On these occasions it required all the authority of the keeper to subdue her resentment.[3]

Another spectator told a similar tale of what had transpired on the night he had seen her perform:

> She was extremely ill, and the man insisted on her dancing, this being one of the tricks which she is forced to display. The poor creature pointed to her throat and to her knees as if she felt pain in both, pleading with tears that he would not force her compliance. He declared that she was sulky, produced a long piece of bamboo,

> and shook it at her: she saw it, knew its power, and, though ill, delayed no longer. While she was playing on a rude kind of guitar, a gentleman in the room chanced to laugh: the unhappy woman, ignorant of the cause, imagined herself the object of it, and as though the slightest addition to the woes of sickness, servitude, and involuntary banishment from her native land was more than she could bear, her broken spirit was aroused for a moment, and she endeavoured to strike him with the musical instrument which she held: but the sight of the long bamboo, the knowledge of its pain, and the fear of incurring it again, calmed her. The master declared that she was as wild as a beast, and the spectators agreed with him, forgetting that the language of ridicule is the same, and understood alike, in all countries, and that not one of them could bear to be the object of derision without an attempt to revenge the insult.[4]

It is clear from these remarks that not everyone in the audience found this kind of entertainment amusing. Within a few weeks, letters of protest began to appear in the London press complaining not only of the degraded nature of the exhibition but also of the state of servitude in which the woman apparently was being kept.[5] Since slavery had recently been abolished in Britain, why was the keeper of this unhappy woman being allowed to profit from her misery? Such a display was both immoral and illegal.

Hendric Cezar responded to this outcry by addressing a rejoinder to the editor of the *Morning Chronicle*:

> Sir,
> Having observed in your paper of this day, a letter signed "An Englishman," containing a malicious attack on my conduct in exhibiting a Hottentot woman, accusing me of cruelty and ill treatment exercised towards her, I feel myself compelled, as a stranger, to refute this aspersion, for the vindication of my own character, and the satisfaction of the public. In the first place, he betrays the greatest ignorance in regard to the Hottentot, who is as free as the English. This woman was my servant at the Cape, and

> not my slave, much less can she be so in England, where all breath [sic] the air of freedom; she is brought here with her own free will and consent, to be exhibited for the joint benefit of both our families. That there may be no misapprehension on the part of the public, any person who can make himself understood to her is at perfect liberty to examine her, and know from herself whether she has not been always treated, not only with humanity, but the greatest kindness and tenderness.
>
> Hendric Cezar[6]

This response provoked more letters to the editor about the show, with some correspondents asserting that Cezar was being less than candid in his remarks and should be compelled to give more details about how he inveigled this woman away from her home and country.[7] One called upon the Missionary Society to intervene on her behalf,[8] and another, "knowing the adventurous hardihood of science," expressed prescient concern lest the woman perish during the winter and then fall into the hands of the anatomists.[9]

Cezar replied again a few days later, offering to show his passport from Lord Caledon, Governor of the Cape of Good Hope, to anyone who cared to see it, and asserting once more that the Female Hottentot was "a subject well worthy the attention of the Virtuoso [sic], and the curious in general...[as] has been fully proved, by the approbation of some of the first Rank and chief Literati in the kingdom, who saw her previous to her being publicly exhibited." He went on to say that he himself no longer took an active part in the exhibition: "as my mode of proceeding at the place of public entertainment seems to have given offense to the Public, I have given the sole direction of it to an Englishman, who now attends." But he also took the opportunity to raise an important new issue by asking if the Hottentot Venus had not "as good a right to exhibit herself as an Irish Giant, or a Dwarf, &c, &c."[10] In other words, wasn't she, like other people in England, at liberty to take up whatever form of employment suited her? Didn't she have a right to work?

Cezar's letter drew a number of angry responses,[11] but only one of these addressed the new issue. Someone signing himself "Humanitas" argued in a long letter to the editor that

> yes, she has a right to *exhibit herself*, but there is no right in her *being exhibited*. The Irish Giant, Mr. Lambert, and the Polish Dwarf, were all masters and directors of their own movements; and they, moreover, *enjoyed, they themselves enjoyed, the profits of their own exhibition*: the first two were men of sound understanding, and were able to tell when *they were plundered and defrauded of these profits, and to insist on the appropriation of exhibition profits to themselves*: the money derived from personal misfortune *was their own*: it comforted them in the active moments of their existence, or supplied them with enjoyment when laid aside. Do the public believe that one shilling, nay a single farthing, of the profits arising from her exhibition will ever go into the hands of the Female Hottentot, or of her relatives or friends? Who audits the accounts? Who looks after the balance between expence and income? the avaricious speculator, or the unfeeling gaoler who have brought her here, who receive the money, and—who will keep it. No; after having run the gauntlet through the three capitals of England, Scotland, and Ireland, and traversed their provincial towns, dragged through them with greater barbarity than Achilles dragged the body of Hector at the foot of his chariot round Troy's walls, this miserable female will be taken back to the Cape; not enriched by European curiosity, but rendered poorer if possible than when she left her native soil.[12]

As these letters make plain, the battle over Sartjee Baartman was shaping up into a classic confrontation between heated humanitarianism and cold commerce, between the abolitionist conscience and the entrepreneurial ideal, between love and money.

The matter was taken to court by three members of the African Institution—Zachary Macaulay, Thomas Gisborne Babington and Peter Van Wageninge—who filed an affidavit at Chancery Lane on October 17th after having seen performances by the Hottentot Venus a few days earlier. Macaulay, explaining that he was Secretary of the African Institution, an organization "the object of which is the civilization of Africa,"[13] said he had gone to Piccadilly on October 11th because he had understood from public advertisements that "a native of South Africa denominated the Hottentot Venus of a most extraordinary and unnatural shape was publicly exhibited for Money" there, and he wanted to find out "under what circumstances she came to England and whether she was made a public spectacle with her own free will and consent or whether she was compelled to exhibit herself." He said that if she wished to return to her own country, the African Institution would be anxious to arrange that she be transported there.

This was no idle boast. Though formed only three years earlier, the African Institution brought together the leaders of the abolition movement in Britain, who collectively could exert a great deal of moral pressure on governmental and religious bodies. Macaulay himself, in addition to his duties as Secretary of this new organization, was then serving on the governing Committee of the Church Missionary Society, and he had been one of the first Governors of the Sierra Leone Colony, which had been formed at the end of the eighteenth century for the purpose of repatriating blacks living in Nova Scotia to a new settlement at Freetown. He was in a good position to marshall support for the repatriation of Sartjee Baartman.

In his affidavit Macaulay described the stage erected in the room in which this woman was exhibited and stated that when she appeared, she "was clothed in a dress resembling her complexion which is very dark and her dress was so tight that her shapes above and the enormous size of her posterior parts are as visible as if the said female were naked and the dress is evidently intended to give the appearance of her being undressed."

He then went on to recount at length the conversation he entered into with Hendric Cezar, who told him that he had obtained her at the Cape of Good Hope from "Dutch Boors" who had come from the interior and that he had been given permission from the Government at the Cape to take her to England. Surprised to hear this, Macaulay asked, "What, did Lord Caledon who is Governor at the Cape give permission for her being brought to England?" Cezar said he did. "Was Lord Caledon's permission in writing?" Macaulay asked. Yes, Cezar replied, it was. "Did Lord Caledon know that she was brought to this country to be exhibited?" Macaulay persisted. "Oh! Yes, Yes," Cezar answered, whereupon Macaulay asked to see the document Lord Caledon had signed, for being in the habit of corresponding with him, he believed he would be able to recognize his handwriting. "What, won't you believe my word?" Cezar responded. "I have already told you that he has signed it and I shall give you no further satisfaction." Macaulay proceeded to ask further questions about the woman but the exhibitor refused to answer them, saying "I do not choose to have so many questions put to me."

In the rest of his deposition Macaulay elaborated on the performance he had witnessed, noting that Cezar "sometimes would call the said female to him, and when she came would desire her to turn round and would invite the spectators to feel her posterior parts...in fact she is exhibited to the public in the same manner that any animal of the brute creation would be exhibited." The woman gave clear signs of being unhappy and dejected, signs that led Macaulay to conclude that she was "under the restraint and control of her exhibitor and is deprived of her liberty." As an example of this, he told of her being ordered to play on a musical instrument "somewhat like a guitar" and displaying evident "mortification and misery at her degraded situation in being made a spectacle for the derision of the bystanders without the power of resistance."

Babington and Van Wageninge, in their part of the joint deposition, testified that at the request of Macaulay they had gone to see a performance by this woman on October 15th and had found it to be exactly as described by him. Van Wageninge, a native of Holland, on being informed by the exhibitor that she could speak imperfect Dutch, put many questions to her ("whence she came, whether she had my relations, whether she was happy and comfortable here, and whether she was desirous of returning home") but she would not answer any of them. Babington and Van Wageninge said they had heard her utter several deep sighs such as would be given by someone whose mind was distressed, and they related the incident in which the curtain was drawn for a moment and the woman threatened with a beating by Cezar for not responding to his commands. They agreed with Macaulay that she was being kept in a condition of involuntary servitude.

On the first of November a supporting affidavit was filed by William Bullock, proprietor of the Liverpool Museum in London, who reported the offer that Alexander Dunlop had made to sell him both a Hottentot woman and a giraffe skin. Bullock, "feeling that such an exhibition would not meet the countenance of the public declined acceding to Mr. Dunlop's proposal and only purchased the skin." In later dealings with Dunlop, Bullock heard him lament being "so unfortunate as to sell and dispose of his Interest in the exhibiting of the said Hottentot Woman and that he has now next to nothing to do with her."[14]

The matter was brought before the magistrates of the Court of the King's Bench on Saturday, November 24th, with the Attorney General pleading on Sartjee's behalf. Since verbatim transcripts of court proceedings were not kept in those days, we must rely on "Law Intelligence" reports in newspapers for an account of what happened when this unusual case was heard. According to *Bell's Weekly Messenger,* the Attorney General's motion asked

> That Mr. Henry [sic] Cezar should shew cause why a Writ of Habeas Corpus should not be directed to him, for the three following purposes—First, to bring up the body of a Hottentot woman, whom he detains, as a public spectacle, in his custody. Secondly, And that he should permit her to be examined by persons cognizant of the language which she understands, whether she is thus detained at her own election, and that such examination should not take place

> in the presence of Mr. Cezar or any of his keepers. Third, To show cause why, at the discretion of the Court, the said female prisoner should not be given up to the charge and protection of the African Institution, they undertaking to give security to the Court, that they will convey her safely back to her own country.[15]

In support of this motion the Attorney General presented the affidavits that had been filed by Macaulay and others representing the African Institution and by William Bullock, and he commented briefly on the disgraceful nature of the performance as well as on the woman's obvious displeasure at displaying herself in so humiliating a manner. At this point one of the magistrates, Mr. Justice Le Blanc, suggested that if the performance was indecent, it would be possible for criminal proceedings to be instituted against Cezar for a breach of public decorum. The Attorney General answered that such was not his present purpose; he sought only an opportunity to ascertain whether the woman was in a state of coercion, and he felt that this could best be done by putting the pertinent questions to her in Dutch in the absence of her keeper but in the presence of court-appointed witnesses for both sides. Some discussion followed as to whether the woman had sufficient command of Dutch to be interviewed in that language, but after being reassured that she appeared to understand Low Dutch, the magistrates felt inclined to rule in favor of this part of the petition.

However, with regard to the third point raised—that the court direct that the woman be transferred from her keeper to the protection of the African Institution—the presiding magistrate, Lord Ellenborough, anticipated a possible legal snag: the court could only restore the liberty of a person held under coercion; it could not transfer this woman to the custody of some other person or group, however benevolent, unless she herself chose to be placed in such custody.

> Before we can remove her from her present situation, we must be satisfied that she is an object capable of making an election: that

> she feels pain from the constraint in which she is at present held; and that she is desirous of being put under the care of persons who will restore her to her own country.[16]

These, then, were the issues to be resolved through an interview in Low Dutch with the woman called the Hottentot Venus. The representatives of the African Institution would be given an opportunity to explain their intentions to the woman so she could make a free choice at the conclusion of the hearing. Lord Ellenborough's reference to "the constraint in which she is at present held" suggests that he may have assumed that the African Institution's assessment of her situation was accurate and would be corroborated by her own statements. Though there were a few small procedural problems remaining, such as the selection of impartial interviewers, the case seemed to be going the abolitionists' way.

The interview took place two days later with the results being reported to the Court on November 28th. Since the deposition made by the witnesses present contains the only testimony we have from Sartjee Baartman herself, and since it includes a number of interesting details, only a few of which were enlarged upon in court, it may be worthwhile to reproduce the entire document here:

> She does not know when she left her native place she being very young when she came to the Cape: the Brother of her late Master, Peter Caesar, brought her to the Cape: she came with her own consent with Peter Caesar and was taken into the service of Henrick Caesar as his nursery maid; she came by her own consent to England and was promised half of the money for exhibiting her person—she agreed to come to England for a period of six years; she went personally to the government in company with Henrick Caesar to ask permission to go to England: Mr. Dunlop promised to send her back after that period at his own expence and to send the money belonging to her with her—she is kindly treated and has every thing she wants; Has no complaints to make against her master or those that exhibit her: is perfectly happy in her present

situation: has no desire whatever of returning to her own country not even for the purpose of seeing her two Brothers and four sisters: wishes to stay here because she likes the Country and has money given her by her Master of a Sunday when she rides about in a Coach for a couple of hours—Her father was in the habit of going with Cattle from the interior to the Cape and was killed in one of those Journeys by the "Bosmen," her mother died twenty years ago—she has a Child by a Drummer at the Cape with whom she lived for about two years yet being always in the employ of Henrick Caesar; the child is since dead—she is to receive one half of the money received for exhibiting herself and Mr. Dunlop the other half—she is not desirous of changing her present situation—no personal violence or threats have been used by any individual against her; she has two Black Boys to wait upon her: One of the men assists her in the morning when she is nearly compleatly attired for the purpose of fastening the Ribbon round her waist—her dress is too cold and she has complained of this to Henrick Caesar who promised her warmer Cloathes; Her Age she says to be twenty two and that her stay at the Cape was three years—To the various questions we put to her whether if she chose at any time to discontinue her person being exhibited, she might do so, we could not draw a satisfactory answer from her—She understands very little of the Agreement made with her by Mr. Dunlop on the twenty ninth October 1810 and which Agreement she produced to us—The time of Examination lasted for about three hours—and the questions put to her were put in such a language as to be understood by her.—and these Deponents say they were informed by the said female that she could neither read or write.

S. Solly
Mr. Geo. Moojen[17]

These unexpected revelations must have astonished the magistrates and the gentlemen of the African Institution, and although there were a few points in the testimony that possibly could have been challenged in court, it was clear from Sartjee Baartman's statements that she completely understood the commercial nature of her contract with Dunlop, that she did not feel pain as a consequence of the conditions of her employment, and that she had no desire to retire from show business or to be placed under the protection of the African Institution. To head off any argument over the point that "she understands very little of the Agreement made with her by Mr. Dunlop on the twenty ninth October 1810," Dunlop had arranged for a Notary Public, Mr. Arend Jacob Guitard, to file a supplementary affidavit stating that he had translated this Agreement from English into Dutch, had read it twice "plainly and distinctly" to Sartjee Baartman and that it had appeared to him "that she understood the contents thereof and was therewith satisfied."[18]

Mr. Gasalee, the defending attorney, then rose to refute some of the charges that had been made against his clients. First, in response to the allegation that Cezar had threatened to strike the woman on stage, Gasalee countered that Cezar no longer took any part in the exhibition so it could not now be claimed that she was being treated cruelly by him before the public. Second, as far as the imputation of indecency was concerned, Gasalee wanted the court to know that during her performance she wore not only a thin silk dress but also a cotton one underneath it. He went on to say that if the African Institution wished to protect her financial interests, his clients would be pleased if they would appoint a trustee to take care of her share in the profits of the exhibition. But since it was evident from her own sworn testimony that the woman was under no restraint, their case against Cezar and Dunlop should be dismissed.[19]

Actually, there was no need for Gasalee to have offered these additional arguments, for the plaintiffs were ready to concede defeat. The Attorney General, admitting that the case against the defendants could not be sustained after the introduction of these new affidavits, summed up by stating that, regardless of the final outcome, anyone who had heard of this action in court must certainly feel that "it was very much to the credit of this country that even a Hottentot could find friends to protect her interests."[20] He trusted that henceforth the woman would be properly taken care of and that "those Gentlemen who had so honourably to themselves taken the trouble of looking into her situation, would continue to see that her interests were protected."[21] As expected, Lord Ellenborough then declared the case dismissed but not before issuing a stern warning that if "any immodest or indecent exposure of this female stranger should take place, those who had the care of her must know that the law would direct its arm with uplifted resentment against the offending parties."[22]

The abolitionists thus lost in court but won in principle. Though they did not manage to close the show down, they do appear to have succeeded in cleaning it up, and Sartjee Baartman may have suffered fewer indignities on stage in the months that followed. Public reaction to the court case was quite positive. One journal exclaimed that "the enquiry does honour to the liberal and humane spirit of our times; to the feelings of the individuals who first instituted it, and to the benevolence of that society by which it was supported."[23] The gentlemen of the African Institution evidently had achieved a moral victory.

Nonetheless, what most impressed ordinary people about the case was not the high conscience of the abolitionists but the low cupidity of the Hottentot. Her insistence upon her right to make a spectacle of herself, like any profit-minded dwarf or giant in the exhibition trade, became the subject of countless jokes, cartoons, and newspaper doggerel. Here is the text of a ballad that began to circulate after the court ruled in her favor:

A BALLAD

The storie of the Hottentot Ladie and her lawfull Knight, who essaied to release her out of captivitie, and what my lordes the Judges did therein.

Oh have you been in London towne,
    Its rareties to see:
There is, 'mongst ladies of renown,
    A most renowned she.
In Piccadillie streete so faire,
    A mansion she has got;

In golden letters written there,
    "THE VENUS HOTTENTOT."

But you may ask, and well, I ween,
    For why she tarries there;
And what, in her is to be seen,
    Than other folks more rare.
A rump she has, (though strange it be,)
    Large as a cauldron pot,
And this is why men go to see
    This lovely Hottentot.

Now this was shewn for many a day,
    And eke for many a night;
Till sober folks began to say,
    That all could not be right.
Some said, this was with her good will;
    Some said, that it was not;
And asked why they did use so ill
    This ladie Hottentot.

At last a doughty Knight stood forth,
    Sir Vikar was his name;
A knight of singular good worth,
    Of fair and courtely fame.
With him the laws of chivalrie
    Were not so much forgot;
But he would try most gallantly
    To serve the Hottentot.

He would not *fight* but *plead* the cause
    Of this most injured she:
And so, appealed to the laws,
    To set the lady free.
A mighty "Habeas corpus"
    He hoped to have got
Including rump and all, and thus
    Release the Hottentot.

Thus driving on with might and main
    This Gallant Knight did say.
He wish'd to send her home again,
    To Afric far away.
On that full pure and holy plan
    To soothe her rugged lot;
[He] swore, in troth, no other man
    Should *keep* his Hottentot.

He went unto the judges grave,
    Whose mercies never fail;
And there, in gallant stile, and brave,
    Set forth the ladie's tale.
He said, a man of cruel heart,
    (Whose name is now forgot,)
Did shew, for pay, the hinder part
    Of this fair Hottentot.

That in this land of libertie,
    Where freedom groweth still,
No one can show another's tail
    Against the owner's will.
And wished my lordes to send some one,
    To know whether or not
This rare exhibiting was done
    To please the Hottentot.

The judges did not hesitate
    This piteous tale to hear
Conceiving her *full-bottom'd* state
    Claimed *their* especial care;
And told the Knight that he might do
    As he thought best, and what;
E'en visit privately, and view,
    His ladie Hottentot.

Then straight two gentlemen they set,

(One English and one Dutch)
To learn if she did money get;
And, if she did, how much.
Who, having finished their intent,
And visited the spot,
Did say t'was done with full consent
Of the fair Hottentot.

When speaking free from all alarm,
The whole she does deride;
And says she thinks there's no great harm
In shewing her b__kside.
Thus ended this sad tale of woe,
Which raised well, I wot,
The fame, and the revenues too,
Of Sartjee Hottentot.

And now good people all may go
To see this wondrous sight;
Both high born men, and also low,
And eke the good Sir Knight.
Not only this her state to mend,
Most anxious what she got;
But *looking* to *her* latter end
Delights the Hottentot.[24]

This ballad, meant as a humorous gloss on a round, unvarnished tale, nevertheless touched upon an aspect of British justice that had very serious implications for Sartjee Baartman—namely, that she could not be protected from exploitation because in ignorance she freely elected to continue working, no doubt believing that she stood to benefit from further self-exposure. Given the opportunity to quit show business, escape from the control of Cezar and Dunlop, and seek repatriation to her homeland, she chose to remain on stage in London. She was willing to collaborate in her own degradation in order to earn more money. Granted she may never have understood exactly what the law suit was all about, and she may have made a fatal error in placing more trust in her managers than in the representatives of the African Institution, but she could not have failed to comprehend what the conditions of her employment were. She had agreed to allow herself to be exhibited indecently to the European public, and she persisted in this tawdry occupation for more than five years, stopping only when her health finally broke down. She may have been the victim of the cruelest kind of predatory ruthlessness, but her collusion in her own victimization is unmistakable. She wanted the show to go on and the profits to keep rolling in. She wanted to capitalize on Western curiosity.

The depths to which she may have been willing to descend to achieve her objective are suggested in a remark made by a French anthropologist when commemorating the one-hundredth anniversary of her death. After a brief review of the career of this notorious celebrity, he said that more than four decades earlier he had heard a scandalous report that "she did not scorn those of her admirers who had the kind of morals that made Sodom famous"; moreover, he felt "compelled to admit that the wax mouldings [of her private parts] in our possession do nothing to contradict these malicious rumors."[25] To put it plainly, she may have engaged in prostitution as well as exhibitionism. Her degradation may have been complete.

But it would be unfair to blame Sartjee Baartman for having fallen into this way of life. She did not fall; she was pushed into depravity by Western opportunists who saw in her a chance to take advantage of Africa's innocence. Promising her a fortune, they lured her into the kind of misery that leads to self-destruction. She may have hoped to become rich by working abroad, but her ultimate reward was an early death. Humanitarian intervention and British justice could not save her from this fate because she swore before witnesses that she was perfectly happy and under no restraint. Taking her at her word, the magistrate presiding over her case was compelled to rule that she could not be emancipated and repatriated because she was already free—and this included being at liberty to make tragic mistakes. Sartjee Baartman, the "Hottentot Venus," had her day in court and lost.

NOTES

1. For further information on her career see Percival R. Kirby, "The Hottentot Venus," *African Notes and News*, 6 (1949), 55-62, and "More About the Hottentot Venus," *Africana Notes and News*, 10 (1953), 124-34; Richard D. Altick, *The Shows of London* (Cambridge, Mass., and London: Belknap Press of Harvard University Press, 1978), pp. 268-72; and Stephen Jay Gould, "The Hottentot Venus," *Natural History*, 91, 10 (1982), 20-27.

2. *Times*, 26 November 1810, p. 3.

3. Mrs. Matthews, *Memoirs of Charles Matthews, Comedian*. Vol. 4 (London: Richard Bently, 1839), p. 137.

4. A Constant Reader, "The Female Hottentot," *The Examiner*, 14 October 1810, p. 653.

5. The first of these, signed "An Englishman," appeared in the *Morning Chronicle*, 12 October 1810, p. 3. A similar letter in *The Examiner* is cited in footnote 17.

6. *Morning Chronicle*, 13 October 1810, p. 3.

7. Humanitas, "Female Hottentot," *Morning Chronicle,* 17 October 1810, p. 3. Following the letter by "A Constant Reader" in *The Examiner* (cited above), the editor added that Cezar's "assertions" in the press "must be listened to with caution, as we have been informed that on her first arrival in London, she was offered for sale by Capt. Cezar."

8. Humanitas, "Female Hottentot," *The Examiner,* 21 October 1810, p. 669. This may be the same "Humanitas" (possibly Zachary Macaulay?) who wrote the letter to the *Morning Chronicle* (cited above) a few days earlier.

9. A Man and a Christian, "The Hottentot Venus," *Morning Post,* 18 October 1810, p. 3.

10. *Morning Chronicle,* 23 October 1810, p. 4.

11. See, e.g., Humanitas, "Female Hottentot," *Morning Chronicle,* 25 October 1810, p. 3., and White Man, "Hottentot Venus," *Morning Post,* 29 October 1810, p. 3.

12. *The Examiner,* 28 October 1810, p. 681.

13. All the remarks by Macaulay, Babington and Van Wageninge quoted here are taken from the Affidavit filed at Chancery Lane (Public Record Office No. KB1/36, pt. 2). It is worth noting that Lord Caledon subsequently denied having a hand in the matter. In a letter to the Earl of Liverpool dated 1 March 1811 he said, "It having been stated in a recent trial before Lord Ellenborough that a female Hottentot had been carried out of this Colony with my knowledge and consent, it is due to the high situation I have the honor to hold, for me to acquaint Your Lordship that I was wholly ignorant of the transaction until long after her departure, and that she never did apply for or receive a permission to leave the Colony." *Records of the Cape Colony from May 1809 to March 1811,* ed. George McCall Theal (Cape Town: Government of the Cape Colony, 1900), Vol. 7, p. 503.

14. Bullock's affidavit (Public Record Office No. KB1/36, pt. 2).

15. *Bell's Weekly Messenger,* 25 November 1810, p. 376. Other accounts of the first day in court may be found in the *Morning Chronicle,* 26 November 1810, p. 3; *Times,* 26 November 1810, p. 3; *Observer,* 25 November 1810, p. 3; and *Morning Post,* 27 November 1810, p. 3.

16. *Morning Chronicle,* 26 November 1810, p. 3.

17. Affidavit signed by S. Solly and Geo. Moojen (Public Record Office No. KB1/36, pt. 2).

18. Affidavit signed by A. J. Guitard (Public Record Office No. KB1/36, pt. 2).

19. Reports of the second day in court can be found in the *Times, Morning Chronicle, Morning Herald, Sun,* and *Courier* of November 29th; *Westminster Journal and Old British Spy* and *Evans and Ruffy's Farmer's Journal* of December 1st; and *Bell's Weekly Messenger, Examiner, News, National Register,* and *Johnson's Sunday Monitor, British and London Recorder* of December 2nd. The case was also widely reported in provincial newspapers, most of which gleaned their stories from the London press. An official summary of the case appears in E. H. East, *Reports of Cases Argued and Determined in the Court of the King's Bench* (London: 1811), pp. 194-95, and this is discussed briefly in "Show Girl—Old Style," *The Solicitor's Journal,* 98 (1954), 545.

20. *Morning Post,* 29 November 1810, p. 3.

21. *Morning Chronicle,* 29 November 1810, p. 3.

22. *Morning Herald,* 29 November 1810, p. 3.

23. "Political Periscope," *The Literary Panorama; Being a Review of Books, Magazines of Varieties, and Annual Register,* 9 (1811), 192.

24. This ballad has been bound between pages 102 and 103 in Volume I of Lyson's unpublished scrapbook of "Collectanea: or, a Collection of Advertisements and Paragraphs from the Newspapers, Relating to Various Subjects" in the British Library. It is reprinted in R. Toole-Stott's *Circus and Allied Arts: A World Bibliography, 1500-1962* (Derby: Harpur, 1962), Vol. 3, pp. 334-36.

25. R. Verneau, "Le centième anniversaire de la mort de Sarah Bartmann," *L'Anthropologie,* 27 (1916), 178. I am grateful to Martin Sonenberg for translating this passage.

Index